T0115011

fresh paint

Add a Splash of Color, Passion and Purpose Back into Your Life!

Kelly Kurtz

BALBOA.
PRESS
A DIVISION OF HAY HOUSE

Balboa Press books may be ordered through booksellers or by contacting:

Balboa Press
A Division of Hay House
1663 Liberty Drive
Bloomington, IN 47403
www.balboapress.com
1 (877) 407-4847

Because of the dynamic nature of the Internet, any web addresses or links contained in this book may have changed since publication and may no longer be valid. The views expressed in this work are solely those of the author and do not necessarily reflect the views of the publisher, and the publisher hereby disclaims any responsibility for them.

The author of this book does not dispense medical advice or prescribe the use of any technique as a form of treatment for physical, emotional, or medical problems without the advice of a physician, either directly or indirectly. The intent of the author is only to offer information of a general nature to help you in your quest for emotional and spiritual well-being. In the event you use any of the information in this book for yourself, which is your constitutional right, the author and the publisher assume no responsibility for your actions.

Any people depicted in stock imagery provided by Thinkstock are models, and such images are being used for illustrative purposes only.
Certain stock imagery © Thinkstock.

Printed in the United States of America.

ISBN: 978-1-4525-1968-5 (sc)
ISBN: 978-1-4525-1969-2 (e)

Library of Congress Control Number: 2014913877

Balboa Press rev. date: 10/28/2014

Dedication

I dedicate this book to the memory of my mother, Vera McCarthy, for the many lessons you taught me and for the inspiration you have given me. I inherited my love of decorating and sense of personal style from you. Writing this book has allowed me to grow into the person I have always been. It is truly a labor of love, for the book you never got to write yourself. Despite missing you each and every day, I smile because I know heaven has a fresh coat of paint now that you are there!

Contents

Acknowledgments..ix

Introduction... xiii

Chapter 1—The Late Bloomer 1

Chapter 2—Finding Your Inspiration 5

Chapter 3—Peeling Back the Layers 21

Chapter 4—Interior Work: Being Grateful............................ 31

Chapter 5—Food and Mood 47

Chapter 6—The Art of Home Staging 69

Chapter 7—Exterior Work: Adding Curb Appeal 95

Chapter 8—The Finishing Touches 109

About the Author 119

Acknowledgments

First, I would like to thank my family for being patient with me as I somewhat secluded myself while writing this book. For my dad and Doris, who lovingly accepted me back "home" without judging me and gave me space and love when I needed it most. Thank you. I wouldn't have made it without you.

To my amazing sister, Robyn, who has been there for me my entire life and who has been my biggest cheerleader. I am so blessed to have you as my sister and best friend.

To my beautiful and talented children, Connor and Kelsey, whose strength and resilience have continually amazed me. I thank God every day for blessing me with the two of you.

You are more than any mother could wish for. You continue to inspire me each and every day.

I would like to thank my dear friend, Steve Stearns, whose countless hours of technical support and friendship made it possible for me to get my words out and saved in my computer, despite many, many glitches. You are incredible and I am lucky to have you as my friend.

For my lifelong friend, Nancy Roberts Roth, whose clever cover design excited me and will catch many an eye. You were patient with me while making it just right through many revisions. Your talent is amazing and to have you play a part in my book project is simply priceless!

To my friend and coach, Jeff St Laurent, who helped me through some dark times years ago. Through life coaching you helped lay the groundwork and allowed me to sort through the many pieces of my life. Perhaps my experiences with you led me to becoming a health coach.

Thanks also to my friend, Karen D'Agostino, who has always believed in me and encouraged me when I wanted to give up.

For my first-round editing team of Kim Kemp Maki and Amy-Jean Cook, I offer my sincere appreciation. You ladies stepped up and assisted me, offered great feedback and incredible generosity of your time and energy. I truly appreciate your honesty and enthusiasm!

For my friend and peer coach, Jennifer Karofsky, who encouraged me to pursue this dream. Saying you couldn't wait to read my book when I hadn't even finished my outline, inspired me to focus and write. You also helped me look through piles of magazines for inspiration and ideas. We will always be friends.

For Wally—your love and support, respect, and kindness have been truly remarkable and truly appreciated. You have been the most amazing father to our two children. We have held true to our mission of being the best parents we can be.

To Joshua Rosenthal and Lindsey Smith from The Institute for Integrative Nutrition—your guidance and confidence kept me going during the many times I doubted myself.

To Dr. Peter Rugg and his wife, Patricia—your enthusiasm and guidance really excited me for the possibilities that are out there even beyond this book!

For my amazing editor, Joni Wilson, whom I have never met in person, but I felt a connection with immediately. Your attention to detail and countless hours and assistance with all my revisions were incredible. This book simply would not have been possible without you!

To Balboa Press, especially Dwight O'Neal, whose very voice got me excited early on to publish with Balboa and Hay House.

Special thanks to the many other friends, coworkers, and family who have supported me throughout this journey. It truly takes a village.

Thank you.

> *If we don't change, we don't grow. If we don't grow, we aren't really living.*
>
> —Gail Sheehy

Introduction

Do you ever look in the mirror and wonder who the heck you are? Have you recently asked yourself just what happened to the person you used to be? Does it seem like just yesterday that you were young and carefree and life flowed easily? If you often feel lost, overwhelmed, or as if you are wandering without direction, you are not alone.

Are you ready for a restoration? A gallon of *Fresh Paint* will get you started. Get ready to rediscover yourself after the years where you adapted, adjusted, and accommodated to meet the needs of others. You did it because you wanted to, or perhaps you needed to, or a combination of both; but either way you did it. You have been patient, unselfish, and loving.

You have carried the torch through thick and thin, and here you are today still holding it. The flame is dimmer and flickering a bit. You might feel as if you are chipping or peeling or have lost your luster. Let the renovations begin! This is your time—your time to embrace, redesign, and celebrate you.

Fresh Paint will teach you simple strategies to rediscover yourself. Find your true colors and passions and redefine your purpose. You will learn ways to increase your self-care, improve your health, nourish your body and soul, and rediscover your unique style. Learn how to keep your brush moving, reclaim and restore peace, tranquility, and serenity in your life. Enjoy the simple abundance.

So, go ahead, read on, your time to sparkle is now!

The change of life is the time when you meet
yourself at the crossroads and you decide
whether to be honest or not before you die.
—Katharine Butler Hathaway

chapter 1
The Late Bloomer

I am 44 years old, sitting in a sun-filled room surrounded by my siblings and my dad. We encircle a hospital bed in a beautiful glass-enclosed room in the house where I grew up. I feel as if I am in a bad dream as we watch my mother take her final breath—just 69 years old when the cancer took her from us. Life is put in perspective when you watch someone you love breathe for the last time.

The final week before Mom died, I spent many hours at her side just watching her sleep and breathe. My sister and I had been sleeping on the floor beside her (on inflatable mattresses) for more than a week, waking every few hours to give her morphine to keep her comfortable. It was during one of the last times we spoke as mother and daughter that we had a special conversation, perhaps one that even inspired me on many levels to write this book.

I remember it vividly: my sister and I were sitting by the bedside, talking and reminiscing. We were lovingly confessing all the times while growing up that we got away with stuff and never got caught. We were laughing. My mother laughed and joked with us and told us that because we were under "special circumstances," we would not be grounded.

My mother then started talking about how she had been a late bloomer. She told us how she was a shy girl who developed into herself through the years; how she overcame self-doubt and learned to truly love herself and embrace life. She honestly loved her family and was truly the cornerstone of ours.

She related how she did things somewhat out of tradition to arrive at where she was in her life. She had no regrets, although she didn't want to miss out on watching all of us as we matured. She had accepted that leaving us physically was inevitable and that her body (which was causing so much pain) was no longer necessary.

Mom believed in heaven and she was anxious to go be with the Lord. She turned to my sister and told her that they were a lot alike. That my sister too was a late bloomer and that many good things were still in store for her. I remember feeling as if they were the lucky ones, that maybe the road less traveled was really the one to be on.

She then turned to me and said, "Kelly, you always knew what you wanted from such an early age (me, who can't make a decision), and you always did everything right. You really were a perfect daughter. You never gave us any trouble; you got good grades, got involved in everything at school and went on to college. You just knew what you wanted; you were driven to be and do and you did it. You graduated, got married to your high school sweetheart, bought a beautiful house, got your master's degree, and have two beautiful children. You truly have it all. You have been a joy to watch and love."

As I listened to her speak, choking back the tears, I realized she was right. I really did follow all the rules. I rarely strayed off course. I did it all the way I thought I was supposed to. So how come, deep inside, I longed for more? I wanted more.

I remember thinking, *I am 44 years old; she is just 69! If I am to share her fate and only make it to 69, I have just 25 years left.* I had twenty-five years to keep being the perfect daughter, the model citizen, and living the vanilla life I believed was my destiny.

Perhaps I had even fooled my own mother and had been untrue to myself. Or maybe that exact conversation, her words and her story, was actually the permission I had been waiting for, to dare to want for something more . . . perhaps at that moment she was teaching me one final lesson, and letting me know that she knew that I too would be a late bloomer after all.

At the center of your being you have the answer:
You know who you are and
you know what you want.
—Lao Tzu

chapter 2
Finding Your Inspiration

Exploring What Calls to You

Have you ever gone into the paint store or the paint section of one of the home improvement stores? There are hundreds, if not thousands, of paint colors and samples. It can be overwhelming if you are not just browsing, but doing a painting project and you actually need to decide on a color.

I am familiar with *50 Shades of Grey,* but who knew there were more than 100 shades of white? The decision can be daunting. Will the color on the teeny-tiny sample look even remotely the same once it is on your wall? Once you pick your hue, there is still the sheen to consider. Do you want eggshell, satin, gloss, semi-gloss, or a designer texture? Do you see where I am going with this? Decisions, decisions, decisions.

Many of us are repainting rooms for the second or even third time if we have lived long enough to do so. Maybe we have recently moved or just simply outgrown the color or we are redesigning our space to accommodate a change in our lives. Life is a lot like paint, a lot like relationships too. It always feels so good, so clean, and so fresh to have a newly painted space. Life, like relationships, is easy to change and often can in a few seconds, by chance or by choice.

I am talking about choice and the power of it. In just a few hours (or even a few minutes), you can change your mind set by selecting your color palate. Even if you pick your color and do nothing else, change within you begins to happen. You start to feel and imagine the color in your space, your life, and your relationships. You might jump a few steps ahead (like I always do) and head on over to your favorite shopping center, where you just happen to find the perfect accessories already waiting for you. It's as if the universe called ahead and said, "She's on her way!"

I am a true believer in the power of desire and intention and manifesting what you want. Whether it is a freshly painted room, running a marathon, landing your dream job, writing a book or finding your soul mate—it can happen, if you can imagine it!

Now that you are interested in getting to know yourself again (or for the first time), take some time to gather a few paint chips. Pick out whatever calls to you. Do you really want to add some color to your life, but your inner voice is talking back to you, saying, *You will be sorry if you go with the yellow* or *The orange is really fun, bold, and funky, but that was you in college, you're different now.* You are a mother (maybe even a grandmother) and you tell yourself, *I am no longer fun and funky,* and out goes the orange. You are drawn to the sea-glass blue, yet your inner voice says, *nice, soothing, and calming,* but this won't match the rest of the house and it really doesn't go with my furniture. And, *Oh, the moss green is really peaceful and serene,* but the gray-and-cranberry carpet you once had to have will look horrible with it.

So you repaint with the same color you always use, or a slight shade lighter to play it safe. You know you need to play it safe, because what if someone thinks the color you pick is too bold or they don't like it? What if your mother or sister gives you that look that tells you they really don't like it, even though they smile and say, "Nice." What if your spouse thinks it's too trendy? And so on and so on. Does this remind you of a pattern of doing what everyone else thinks you should, rather than what your instincts tell you that you want? Go ahead, its only paint!

You see this book is about painting—color and restoration. Yet it's not really about actual painting. It's about many things— your talents, your desires, your interests, and your passions in all areas of your life. It's about asking yourself questions and listening to the answers already within you.

I like the similarities it has with painting because I often envision myself with a paintbrush as I am moving along my journey. I know that paint is easy to change. If you make a mistake, it's not permanent. You can always change. It takes the pressure off being perfect and making a "wrong" decision. You can change your paint color. Start with a paint chip, sample with a small brush, then transition to a bigger brush or even a roller. If you are really diving in, heck you can even try a paint sprayer! Exploring, imagining, and then doing! Truly exhilarating! Taking small steps forward to see how it looks, feels, and rejuvenates you.

If this sounds a bit overwhelming and you just don't know how or where to start, I have a great exercise that you can do. It is fun and it really works. It is called a dream board. You may have heard of it or even created one before. It is a wonderful collage of sorts. We have all probably had to make one at some point in our lives—maybe when we were in school or helped our kids with one. The difference is this one is yours, and yours alone. So pick a time and just do it.

You can work alone or ask a friend to join you. Get out the scissors and a glue stick. Feel like a kid again. Start with a foam-backed poster board or even a sheet of paper. I recommend the poster board, because you need room for your dreams. A bigger board allows more creative space to explore. You can do what feels right for you. Remember you can always make another board, and you should, as your dreams turn to realities.

Getting Started

- foam-backed poster board
  (gives more substance than the flimsy ones)
- glue stick or craft glue
- magazines
- brochures
- photos

Start sifting through the magazines, brochures, and photos you have. It's a scavenger hunt of sorts, an archaeological dig; you never know what you might uncover. Cut out whatever calls to you—whatever catches your eye or moves your spirit. It can be a color, an outfit, a hairstyle, a beautiful item in a sun-filled room, words, or something personal to you. How about a couple walking along the beach holding hands or a porch or patio filled with people laughing and enjoying themselves on a summer afternoon.

My point is there really are no rules. You are your life's general contractor. So choose anything—anything at all. We often don't have or take the time to browse and really look at what's before us. Yes, we have all flipped through a magazine or two while waiting for the dentist or doctor. This is similar, yet different. Ask yourself when the last time was that you sat quietly with a pile of magazines and a cup of your favorite beverage. Now add your favorite music and you are on your way!

Once you have your inspirations, glue these things on your board. Fill it up with whatever inspires you. Use words, pictures, fabrics, or anything at all. Then hang it up! Don't stick it in the basement behind boxes of storage where you will never see it again. Put it somewhere where you can see it often. It could be in your home office, on your closet door, even on your refrigerator. The point is to release your intentions and dreams to the universe. Once they are out there in plain sight, you begin manifesting all that you desire.

I have done several of these through the years, and I am always amazed at how they play themselves out when I rediscover past boards. The similarities are truly amazing and powerful. I am not saying they happen overnight and that I posted a picture of a million dollars and now I have it, but the things I have truly desired have come into my life. As I know what I focus on and intend to receive, those desires seem to find their way to me.

In addition to the dream board, I find that journaling has a real place in helping me rediscover myself. I know in the past there have been times when I have thought about what I have written, and I panic at the thought of someone reading my journal entries. What would he or she think or say? It's somewhat like the *Brady Bunch* episode when Jan reads Marsha's diary.

The benefit of free-style writing is amazing and your thoughts and emotions can truly pour out of you. It is extremely therapeutic. I have come to realize that those journal entries are meant for me and me alone. No one really cares or will take the time to read my journal. It is sacred space for me and it can be for you.

Keep your journal somewhere that is your personal space. Select a journal that calls to you. It can be as simple as a spiral notebook, a lime green leather-bound book, or a bedazzled binder. Whatever you choose, it is yours and yours alone. I also suggest getting a pen that just feels great in your hand, one that writes smoothly and effortlessly. You deserve a pen that allows you to channel your thoughts to the paper. Who knows—maybe there is a book waiting to be written inside you.

For some of us, our dreams have been clear for as long as we can remember. We have always known what they are. For others of us, our dreams evolve, develop, and take shape over time. It is OK to not know what you ultimately want, it truly is a process.

How many times have you heard an inspirational story of a person who started out on one path and ended up on another? Life can seem like it is shattered instantly when our dreams don't happen exactly the way we had planned.

Sometimes our shortfalls are our greatest moments. Author Mitch Albom reminds us that, "All endings are also beginnings, we just don't know it at the time." I challenge you to create what sets your heart ablaze. You will find your way, as all our paths are a little bit different.

I had recently gone through a divorce after my mother died. I was married for more than 20 years. For financial reasons, I found myself temporarily moving back to live with my dad. He lived just a mile away and had enough room for me and my two teenage children. Living there allowed them to be close enough to their dad so he and I could share joint custody of our two amazing kids. So, I moved back into the house where I grew up and got my old room back. This was the first time in my life, with the exception of my last two years of college that I had ever had my own room. Growing up I shared a room with my sister.

The first few months were tough. I felt like I was living in a foreign space, even though it was so familiar to me. The decor had changed during the years since I left the nest—from twin beds, bulletin boards with high school memories, and posters of teen heartthrobs adorning the walls. My new space contained my grandmother's antique bed and some simple, beautiful, antique pieces that my parents had lovingly collected through the years.

It was strange to be an adult daughter living with my dad again. I was trying to remember that I was in my 40s and not a teenager like I was when I last lived there. I wasn't going to get grounded and didn't have to ask permission to stay out past curfew. The funny thing is the roles were somewhat reversed.

I was home and in bed by nine most every night. I was leaving the outside lights on for him!

After I came to accept that I would likely be living there for a while, until things would settle for me, I felt compelled to transform the space to reflect more of me. I had owned three houses during my 20-plus years of marriage and had taken pride in decorating and making them comfortable for my family. Now I was starting fresh in many ways.

Sorting through the broken pieces, I considered that first year of transition to be a 1,000-piece puzzle. I often imagined myself sitting on the floor among the pieces scattered all around me, often feeling overwhelmed, shocked, and sad. So many pieces, where to start? I had always started a giant puzzle with the edges and worked my way in, so that was how I approached this situation.

I spent many hours reflecting, crying, and riding my bike mile after mile—riding away from the pain and riding toward the unknown. Looking back now, I know that days, weeks, and months went by that I don't really remember. I was not truly present. I was so involved in reliving the past and worrying about the future that I really lost track of time. I remember pieces and moments of that first year that my marriage ended, but I spent most of my hours in my room. With the exception of going to work, being with my kids, or being on my bike, I took a giant time out. It felt somewhat like solitary confinement.

It was during this first year that I began to transform from the inside out. I used my journaling to get through some dark times. Slowly I began to transform my new room to a place of peace and tranquility. I kept the fresh clean canvas of the white walls and the antique white coverlet that was already on the bed. I started with a few new toss pillows for my bed. I added a beautiful soft throw to the foot of the bed for comfort and warmth during the many naps I took whenever I couldn't bear to be in the world awake. I rediscovered my favorite store, TJMaxx, and picked up small simple accessories that called to me, like treasures.

I sorted through my clothing, my jewelry, and my books. What did I absolutely love and couldn't live without? What could I donate or give away that was just "stuff"? I began to use positive daily affirmations and created a Pinterest account. I allowed myself to dream again—to begin to realize that everything might be OK—that I was strong and that if I could just take it one day at a time I could make it. So I forged on.

Slowly I began to freshen up the bathroom that I was using. I changed the shower curtain, splurged on some nice shampoo and conditioner and even bought a new bathrobe. These small, simple, inexpensive things made me feel good. I had abandoned my authentic self for so long, and now I started to feel better in my own skin. The puzzle border was taking shape, and I could sort the pieces into colors and sections.

I began to organize my dad's pantry, and I created my own shelf of things. I knew I needed to return to cooking for myself when I was alone and without the kids. I needed to nourish my body like I was learning to nourish my soul—one meal at a time, one day at a time. I always was intrigued by the power of food. I had been an emotional eater most of my adult life. Although I had been thin to average growing up, my weight had waffled up and down during the years.

Looking back, my weight correlated with my moods and happiness or lack thereof. As I sorted through my closet of clothes, I realized that I had been nearly 40 pounds heavier a few years back. As I moved through this transition, I had been shedding layers of sadness and despair. I knew food was a powerful drug that seemed to follow my moods, and I realized I was not alone and that other women had been on similar journeys.

I felt compelled to share what I was learning and help others. It was at that moment that I decided I would become a holistic health coach. I had wanted to for quite some time, but it was expensive and my husband and I were committed to our children and had them in private schools. With college approaching in their near future, it wasn't a priority for me to take on anything new.

But now, at the age of 45, for the first time in my life I was able to make decisions for myself. I was scared and had many conversations with that inner voice inside my head. It had lots of negative self-talk for me: *You don't deserve this, you are not good enough, and what will people think?*

The desire outweighed the fear. I had some personal financial rearranging to do, but I paid off my debt and enrolled in The Institute for Integrative Nutrition to become a Certified Health Coach. I also bought an iPad, which allowed me to complete my coursework, connect with the world, and finally get on the Pinterest site that everyone was raving about.

Pinterest was my catalyst for dreaming—fashion, health, wellness, decorating, and dreaming about a new home. I could let my imagination run wild. The possibilities were endless. I could pick and choose whatever called to me. I could save pictures on my own boards (sort of like a dream board of intentions that we talked about before) and they became my happy place—the place between where I was currently and where I wanted to go. I had a vision, an end line. I just needed to move in the direction I wanted to go.

Those three things, getting debt free, pursuing a career that inspired and excited me, and the iPad really started the ball rolling for me. For the first time in my life, I listened to my instincts, took a leap of faith, and took action toward creating the life I was longing for.

So I guess that was the first layer I had to uncover—like stripping wallpaper or selecting a paint color. It took a lot of thinking, pondering, and changing my mind set. I was afraid to make the first tear in the wallpaper. It seemed as if I kept looking at the corners, studying the seams to see if and where I should start. And then it happened. I grabbed a piece and started tearing.

I was surprised at how easy the first piece came down, then another, and still another. Was this possible? Had I been terrified all along only to realize it wasn't so bad? Was it the fear that had been holding me back all along? Well, yes and no. I started to hit some tough spots, and, yes, I had a few panic attacks. What had I done? What was I thinking? I was in between with no chance to go back, and the only way was to forge ahead. So I did, one piece at a time.

So I ask you, What layers are hiding just below your surface? What are you longing to uncover and expose? What part of your authentic self are you running from? Some of us truly know, others may not, yet still many are pretending not to know. I ask you to take a moment, think, and ponder. Listen to your inner voice and tell it to take a time out. There is plenty of time for that voice, but not now. Now is the time to hear what you are saying in your heart and soul. What are you longing for? What is calling to you? Many of us never give way to those thoughts as we self-sabotage before they can ever really be thought out.

Remember the term daydreaming? I think we use to do a lot more of that before we had Smartphones, texting, iPads, and computers everywhere. Think about it. When do you ever have a chance to just be, to listen to silence, and let your mind wander? I believe that people who run, bike, walk, and swim for exercise have opportunities many of us don't. You see those activities usually require extended time—time that is often spent alone.

I will say that if you have ever run several miles, run a marathon, or biked 20, 30, 50, or 100 miles, you probably know what I am talking about. Perhaps cycling and swimming are the best, because those are activities in which you are not likely to be wearing headphones. When you are alone with yourself in nature, you have time to embrace the beauty, smell beautiful things, listen to the birds, and even hear yourself breathe.

In 2011, I was training for the Pan-Mass Challenge, a 192-mile, two-day, cycling event that raises money for the Jimmy Fund and the Dana-Farber Cancer Institute in Boston, Massachusetts. My training consisted of three to four 20–25- mile rides in the early morning before work. The weekends would entail my longer rides consisting of 50, 60, or 80-mile rides. During these mid-week rides, I would leave my house by 5:15 a.m. and ride 20–25 miles before most people had gotten out of bed or had a cup of coffee.

Those mornings were so therapeutic to me in many ways. It was just me out on the bike, no one to answer to except myself—no music, no cell phone, no TV, no computer, and no distractions. There were just the birds, an occasional deer or fox, many squirrels, and me. I would occasionally pass a runner or see another cyclist, and we would wave or nod, like a code for "Yeah, you got it too."

That peaceful feeling is like nothing I have ever experienced. Yes, there were mornings when it was chilly, or I was sore or just plain tired. There were days when I remember most every pedal stroke and other days I don't remember how I got home—different levels of thought. I laughed, I cried, I was sad, happy, angry, empowered, free, strong, and determined. I had many conversations with myself on the bike and, yes, many with other people, even though I was alone! It was a time just for me, a place to think and grow. It was truly therapeutic and I can honestly say my bike rides changed my life. What are you longing for? What is inside of you to discover and bring you peace and joy?

Looking back, I think the time on my bike was like clearing my space. It's like when you are first moving to a house or an apartment and it is empty. Like a clean slate in your mind, you can start to visualize where things will go. Starting with a clean canvas allowed me to let more of my inner voice speak, to listen to my authentic self because I allowed it time and space to reemerge.

What form of exercise or meditation are you currently practicing, if any? Gym memberships are nice and often essential in order to get in a workout. However, I challenge you to think about picking a form of exercise that is also meditative that can help you expose your bare walls. Go ahead and try it, even if it is one or two times a week. Go alone and see what that solitude can do for you.

Just when the caterpillar thought the
world was over, it became a butterfly.
—A Proverb

chapter 3
Peeling Back the Layers

As my remodel project was evolving, I continued to liken it to peeling back the layers of wallpaper. If you have ever lived in an old house, you know what I am talking about. Some of the paper peels off easily and then there are patches that are stubborn. You can chisel, scrape, pick, and peel, and it seems like certain areas just won't budge.

Throughout the years, I had periods of honest-to-goodness, elbow-grease rehabbing and periods of band-aid patching and covering up imperfections. There were also some dark times where I went through the motions with my smile stuffed in my pocket as I walked out into the world. I had gotten fairly good at autopilot. In fact, that was the place where I was most comfortable.

At the age of seven, I was repeatedly molested by a priest who was considered to be a family friend. It was "our secret" and one I would keep from everyone, including my parents, friends, and family until I was 23 years old.

When I reflect on my journey thus far, I have many instances that I thought, *Why did this happen to me?* At the time, I was in my victim mindset. Being in that mindset was actually quite easy because I didn't need to hold myself accountable. I could give up time and time again and always have an excuse that was valid. After all, I was damaged goods, or so I came to believe.

My experience as a child turned me away from the Catholic church, and in doing so, I lost my relationship with God and my faith faltered. I spent years in anger, rage, and lost love and gratitude. Behavioral science author Steve Maraboli, who wrote *Life, the Truth, and Being Free,* says, *At every given moment we are absolutely perfect for what is required for our journey.* This means having faith that you will not be given more than you can handle, even when it feels like you have been robbed of your very soul.

I tell you this not to gain your sympathy but to show you that years of running from yourself will catch up with you sooner or later. When you feel badly about yourself, you lose your basic self-esteem. I became really good at keeping my secret and mastered the appearance of being polished on the outside, when in fact I was I really peeling on the inside. I was always "sprucing" up all around me and trying to be a really good mother, daughter, and wife.

Many days I dreamed about what it must be like to be happy. Emotions such as joy, peace, harmony, and tranquility were simply words to me. I wasn't sure of what those true emotions were, but I imagined feeling them would be nothing short of amazing. There were times when I got scared and panicked at the thought of, *What if this is it? What if true happiness doesn't even exist?* I often pondered the realization of *How will I know if I get there?*

Along my journey, I have come to remember a quote that often runs through my head in times like these, which says, "Sometimes a change of self is often needed more than a change of scene." It is easy to run, to hibernate, and to seclude yourself. You learn to avoid people, places, and things, and to distance yourself from the perceived pain that you come to expect.

I often experience the feeling like I am living in a glass-enclosed cube. This is my safe spot. It allows me to see what is going on and people can see me, but no one is allowed close enough to touch or penetrate the walls.

Do you have walls around you? If so, describe how they serve you. How do they keep you from living in the present moment?

_____

_____

_____

_____

_____

How do the walls keep you from moving forward?

_____

_____

_____

_____

_____

Embracing the Imperfections

Simply put an imperfection is a blemish, a defect, or a flaw. For years, I had lists of all the things I didn't like about myself. I dreamed that if I were rich enough one day, I would begin having them repaired, remodeled, and redesigned. I would take one area at a time and just simply get it fixed. I was correlating my physical body with happiness of my soul and spirit.

I truly believed that if I looked a certain way, saw an ideal number on the scale, or viewed a specific silhouette in the mirror, then those things would buy me happiness. I saw it purely as a money problem, or lack thereof. I was fooling everyone with my Oscar, Grammy, and Emmy award-winning performances on the outside. No one could ever tell the shabby self-esteem and ghetto poverty I felt within.

My belly had stretch marks, and the varicose veins along my legs were like road maps. Excess weight made me look bloated and uncomfortable in my own skin. A lack of daily energy was my normal. I had lost my sparkle. When you do not like what you see in the mirror, your everyday body language reflects that which is within.

I knew I needed the "change-of-self" quote I spoke of earlier. Small, simple steps moving in the direction I desired were all I could commit too. I was motivated and inspired by Anthony Robbins and Dr. Wayne Dyer, my two new best friends. I decided to use the power of visualization to imagine the body I wanted.

Learning self-love began with accepting that the belly that was no longer firm and flat had given me two amazing children, and the varicose veins were a result of those back-to-back pregnancies. I started to view them as a sacrifice of myself for having received the gift of two amazing and healthy children. When put in that perspective, I wouldn't trade them for my version of perfection.

I started to focus more on the things I could control, such as shedding the excess weight. Through the help of my life coach, Jeff St Laurent, I began to view food as nourishment that would fuel and replenish my body so that I could move and embrace the life I was given. I was punishing myself by eating highly processed, sugar-laden foods because I didn't feel worthy of the time and energy it took to plan and prepare healthy and nutritious meals.

I did not value myself enough to commit to daily exercise, basic self-care, and a daily meditation practice. Once I changed my mindset and knew that these essentials were part of my 1,000-piece puzzle, I embraced them and fit them into my mosaic.

What imperfections are you struggling with?

_____

_____

_____

_____

_____

How can you view them differently to make them uniquely yours?

_____

_____

_____

_____

_____

The Power of Paint

Up until now, I have been talking about various colors of paint. Let me share with you a story about body art and tattoos. One day I was talking with a coworker who had lost more than 200 pounds during a six-year period. An incredible feat, she looked simply amazing.

We were at dinner one evening with a group of folks from work, and she was talking about the tattoos she had covering her upper arms and shoulders. I was asking her some questions about her weight loss and about the tattoos. I asked her why she chose to put them there. What she told me next really resonated with me.

She said that after she lost so much weight, her skin was saggy and even though she was wearing smaller clothes, she was still self-conscious because of the stretch marks on her arms. The tattoos were of beautiful colored flowers, and she chose them as a way to add beauty to the body she had renovated. Thus, her stretch marks became a sign of inner strength and beauty— an offering of transforming beauty to the body that she had reclaimed and restored.

The first hope of a painter who feels hopeful about painting is the hope that the painting will move, that it will live outside its frame.

—Gertrude Stein

What areas are you covering up? What imperfections are defining you? How can you practice self-love and embrace the unique, strong and powerful individual you are?

_____

_____

_____

_____

_____

Perhaps self-love has been the biggest challenge and greatest obstacle for me personally. It is likely one that I fear I will never truly conquer. Yet I know it holds the key to so many things that lie ahead. It has been a roadblock, a detour, even an avalanche at times. It has been a fierce hurricane, a powerful and devastating tsunami, and an explosive earthquake all rolled into one, one great big natural disaster.

There is always a recovery, a period of rebuilding, and an awakening that occurs when self-love and self-esteem are shattered. It takes time but it happens like the ebb and flow of the tide. When it is lost, it searches and yearns to be found, embraced and finally reignited.

I have often read that you will never fully love someone until you truly love yourself and that alone frightens me. In fact, psychologist Rollo May says, *Self Love is not only necessary and good, it is a prerequisite for loving others.* If I cannot conquer loving myself, how can I expect to find the true love I am seeking?

I often turn to quotations and affirmations when I need gentle reminders that, *Life is too short to be at war with yourself.* Buddha reminds me that, *You, yourself, as much as anybody in the entire Universe, deserve your love and affection.*

Once I regain my balance and become increasingly more energized, I remind myself of the words of poet Oscar Wilde, *To love oneself is the beginning of a lifelong romance.* Now, doesn't that sound magnificent?

What new and exciting relationship are you ready to begin with yourself? How can you unpeel the layers of your wallpaper to transform the vision of yourself and allow beauty to radiate from within?

Mark Twain's powerful words remind us, *The worst loneliness is to not be comfortable with yourself.*

*I have found that worry and irritation
vanish the moment I open my mind to the
many blessings I possess.*
—Dale Carnegie

chapter 4
Interior Work: Being Grateful

Procrastination and Self-Sabotage

Sound familiar? Procrastination is defined by Wikipedia as "the practice of carrying out less urgent tasks in preference to more urgent ones, or doing more pleasurable things in place of less pleasurable ones, and thus putting off impending tasks to a later time." Here comes that quest to be perfect again. You are afraid of making a mistake or a bad decision that you maybe will later regret.

One thing I know about is that you have the right to change your mind! You can come to realize that every decision you make isn't set in stone forever. Take those serious decisions more seriously and use strategies like I have mentioned, such as getting in touch with your inner voice to guide you on which way to go.

You probably remember Little Orphan Annie from the musical by the same name and her famous line, "The sun'll come out tomorrow" from the song "Tomorrow." I often think of this and realize, yes, the sun will be out again. Maybe some rain, wind, sleet, and snow will pass by first, but "bet your bottom dollar that tomorrow there'll be sun." You see, being gray happens to us all.

Do you find yourself living in the past, dwelling on the mistakes you made? I have spent much time there myself. In fact there are years of my life that I remember only vaguely, because I was living in the past for most of them.

The concept of being present or living in the present moment is not a new one. Yet, it is difficult for many of us. Have you ever met someone who just has endless energy? It's the kind that radiates to everyone they come in contact with. They seem happy and see the glass as half full most or all of the time.

Those people usually live in the present moment. They have learned or truly believe that they must move on each and every day. They see their shortcomings as merely "bumps in the road." They know that today is a new day, and that each new day brings innovative and better things that can happen. When you can find that space, life truly begins to change.

Robert T. Kiyosaki writes, *It is not what you say out of your mouth that determines your life. It is what you whisper to yourself that has the most power.* Not believing that my voice mattered made for many, many years of being a prisoner in my own life.

Self-Sabotage

Sabotaging occurs when we find ourselves creating problems that will interfere with our goals. Some of the common behaviors can include forms of self-medication, such as alcohol, excessive shopping, and overeating foods that make us "feel good," therefore the term "comfort food." We will talk more about those feel-good foods later in the book, as the power of food is simply amazing.

Somehow, we truly want what we are trying to achieve, but again that voice in our heads tells us, *You don't deserve this, You can't do it, You are not good enough.* Sometimes we are more afraid of success than we are of failure, because failure is more acceptable. It is often easier to say, "I tried that, it was awful," or "That diet is ridiculous, no one can survive that," or "I just don't have time to train for the Boston Marathon, my kids and husband need me." More people can relate to failures, because we have all shared in them.

Take a moment and think about ways in which you might be procrastinating and sabotaging yourself. Jot them down now. Write whatever comes to mind that you find yourself doing that is getting in the way of what you want and deserve.

_____

_____

_____

_____

_____

Waiting for Perfect

Do you suffer from the quest for perfectionism? I was the master at it. I think it is also called obsessive-compulsive disorder. I have spent most of my life getting my ducks in a row, so to speak. Organizing, planning, sorting, cleaning, clearing, and re-doing to get things just right. I have always looked for what's next.

If I just do this, or that, or get this degree or that certification then, finally then, I will be happy and complete. If I can get my home office organized with bright colors and cool desk accessories then my business will grow because I will be "ready." How about "if I just re-do the bathroom and the kitchen, then my house will be just right and I can invite friends over, which will lead to meaningful relationships." Or "Maybe if I just lose

20 pounds then I will buy beautiful clothes and look amazing and have all the self-confidence I need to land that new job."

Does this sound familiar? Are you unable to see the forest through the trees? I have learned that sometimes all we want and need is what we already possess within us. We are just afraid to allow it to manifest itself.

I often think back to my amazing grandmother. During her final year of life, she was in a nursing home. One day she told me how happy and lucky she was to be living there. She told me that she had such a good life. She had been an orphan at the age of six, when both her parents had died. She moved from Canada to Massachusetts to live with her older brother and his new wife. She had a hard life by today's standards. Yet, she truly saw the glass as half full.

One day I stopped in to see her and she thanked me for helping her live there. She said with a big smile, "I have everything here that I need. I have clean sheets, a fresh bar of soap, and a pitcher of nice cold water." That was it. That made her happy with a kind of simple abundance that I will never forget. Simply amazing.

I have a seen an anonymous quote that goes something like this, "Some of the things we take for granted each and every day can be someone else's prayers just waiting to be answered." That is the truth.

What are some of the basic things you already have in your life that you are grateful for?

_____

_____

_____

_____

_____

The Gratitude Jar

Around the time I was organizing my new "room" at my dad's house, I came across a nice, big, glass jar. The lid had broken and the jar was just sitting there in his pantry. I was drawn to it for some reason and thought I wanted to bring it upstairs and put it on my bureau. It sat there for a few days empty, just waiting to be filled with something.

My first thought was to put my collection of heart-shaped rocks in it. They were all so unique and really needed to be displayed in a different way. Then when I was getting a scrap piece of paper to jot down a phone number, it dawned on me. I had a nice little memo pad that had two colors of paper on it—blue and green. I had picked it up at a dollar store, because I had been drawn to the colors that reminded me of sea glass.

Immediately I took a sheet of the blue paper and wrote on it, "**I am grateful for my Dad and for the safe, comforting space that I have here in his home.**" I folded the paper neatly in half and then in half again and placed it in the jar. Just like that my Gratitude Jar was born.

Each evening before going to bed, I would write down something I was grateful for. It ranged from a hug and a kiss from my daughter, to the delicious salad I had for lunch to the **"love you too"** text from my son. As I began to add things to my jar, something amazing began to happen. I started to become more present in the moment. I started to notice more of the little things I had taken for granted for so long.

> *I try to be grateful for the abundance of the blessing that I have, for the journey that I'm on, and to relish each day as a gift.*
> —James McGreevey

I was reminded of my grandmother and the things she was grateful for. I am astounded at my Gratitude Jar today. It sits on my bureau in my beautiful condo and is a colorful reminder of all the wonderful things in my life, adding another dimension to my painting.

The abundance I already have, here and now. Those are the things that matter most. It's not how much money I have or that my stairs need to be vacuumed or the dishwasher needs unloading. It's the daily reminders that we often have all that we need while we continue to pursue more of what we want.

Do you have difficulty accepting compliments? Do you feel unworthy of them, and before you can respond a voice steps in with a sarcastic and negative reply?

> *Perhaps in receiving we heal others; in giving we heal ourselves.*
>
> —Unknown

What are some of the gifts (compliments) you have received lately?

_____

_____

_____

_____

_____

Did you accept them with a smile, or dismiss them and not fully receive?

Getting Started

Find yourself a jar or container that calls to you to become your Gratitude Jar. I recommend one that is clear so you can see your abundance easily. Pick out some pretty paper or index cards. Get creative if you want to by using pretty scrap-booking paper cut into squares with pinking shears for added texture, color, and interest. Write away. Before you know it, your Gratitude Jar will be full of the simple treasures that surround you.

Shades of Gray

If you are like most people, you have had days in your life when you feel down. Many refer to it as having the blues. But to me, blue is such a serene color and all shades of blue (from navy to the palest of blue skies) don't correlate to sadness to me, but gray does. Especially after I turned 40, when the gray hairs began to show up in full force!

Gray, even in its palest form, is neutral to dull and somewhat lacking in feeling. Then there is battleship gray that is solid and endless. Taylor Swift sings, "You paint me a blue sky, And go back and turn it to rain." I love that line and really can relate to it. The trick is to have more blue skies than rain in your life and perhaps the key is to be able to turn your own gray to blue. I believe we can.

Have you ever felt like the sadness might not ever end? Sometimes day after day of feeling down, gives little to make you smile. I can remember talking to my children when they were younger and sad about something. We would often talk it through and then I would say, "OK, now let's turn that frown upside down." We would smile, sometimes slowly at first, but it usually would work. The lesson in all of it wasn't to *not* feel your feelings but instead to realize that by taking that one action of making yourself smile, you could literally begin to change the way you feel.

I think that is so powerful when you realize that you, yes you, have the power to change not only how you feel but how you respond to situations with your conscious effort and energy. Yes, easier said than done sometimes. There are plenty of times when you need to let it all go and cry your eyes out.

Here is a little prayer, written by Ralph Waldo Emerson, that I often say at bedtime: *For each new morning with its light, for rest and shelter of the night, for health and food, for love and friends, for everything Thy goodness sends.*

fresh paint

For many years, I did not allow myself to feel feelings that were sad or angry. I tried to be happy, or at least appear to be, if anyone was around. I would get quiet, not make a fuss, and essentially go unnoticed whenever I felt something I was uncomfortable with. I didn't like to fight. Some call it the middle-child syndrome or the peacemaker. Can you relate? Where do you fit in, in your family?

The lack of fighting turned out to be an imperfection that I would have to work on most of my adult life. I lost my voice along the way, and use to think that everyone else's opinion was more important than my own. I was agreeable, easy to get along with, and became wishy-washy.

Making decisions was stressful for I feared making the wrong choice. Even something as simple as being asked, "Where do you want to go for dinner?" would usually result in an automatic, "I don't care, I'm up for anything," or "Wherever you want is fine." This is just a small example, but the point I am making is that I gave up my choices, put my feelings aside, and did not value myself enough to say what I wanted.

I became passive and complacent. I spent years going with the flow with anger, bitterness, and disappointment simmering on low in the Crockpot for years. Do you have feelings left on the stove? Do they simmer on low then finally boil over? Or do yours ignite like gasoline in a flame?

Close your eyes and choose a color that comes to mind for your sadness. Describe how that color makes you feel.

_____

_____

_____

_____

_____

Now think of a color that you love. One that makes you feel good all over. Can you add some of that color into your everyday life? Maybe it is a scarf, a sweater, or perhaps a pair of earrings. Maybe it is a coffee mug that you start off with each and every morning.

What color are you going to use and how can you provide a reminder to feel good about yourself?

_____

_____

_____

_____

_____

As I mentioned earlier, I am a big fan of Taylor Swift. Even though I am more than twice her age, I feel I can relate to many of her song lyrics. Her latest album *Red,* with a song by the same name, uses colors to illustrate feelings. The song says, "Losing him was blue like I'd never known, Missing him was dark grey all alone, Forgetting him was like trying to know somebody you've never met, but loving him was red." Have you ever experienced red?

Daily Affirmations

Do you have any quotes or sayings you use on a regular basis? There are some positive ones and probably several negative ones that you might not even be aware of. One negative quote that comes to mind for me is, "I can never have anything nice." That's really a terrible saying.

You see if you repeatedly tell yourself something, you eventually begin to believe it. That is true on so many spectrums. The mindset here is saying *I don't deserve nice things.* However, I believe we all deserve nice things in general. Expecting gloom and doom sends negative energy to the universe. Don't you deserve better? You must plant your own garden and water your own soul to truly cultivate all that you deserve and desire.

The affirmations I want us to focus on are positive ones that promote and encourage self-love and affection.

In order to be loved completely and deeply, we must love our selves first. That is often easier said than done. In a society of constant comparison, we can easily feel like we fall short of being all that we want and desire. How many times have you compared yourself to someone's great photo, vacation, or comment about how amazing their life is? I encourage you to take it with a grain of salt, because as we know, if you have to brag about how great you are, chances are you are embellishing a bit. Realize that those snippets are likely not a real portrayal of life.

Louise Hay is one of my favorite authors. She uses a lot of positive daily affirmations in her writings and I like that. A good friend of mine took the time to write several of them out for me on pretty colored index cards—one affirmation per card.

I select one at a time and display it on my dresser in my bedroom. I read it every morning and before I go to bed until it feels right. Sometimes I change it daily and other times I stay on one particular affirmation for several days and then change it. You can do the same thing with your index cards or sticky notes. Get creative. Put them where you need a reminder—your mirror, your car, your refrigerator, your computer, etc. Setting your intention to love yourself truly sets the tone for the day, the week, and your life. Here are a few of my favorites:

"I believe in my ability to guide myself in the right direction."

"I enjoy my body and all the pleasures it brings me with delight."

"I trust my inner voice and my intuition to show me the way."

"I love the person that I am as well as the one that I am becoming."

Take a moment and write down a few affirmations that resonate with you.

_____

_____

_____

_____

_____

Keep the Paint Brush Moving

By now, you probably realize the similarities between painting and blooming. The process of finding our authentic selves is not only discovery but also cultivating, nurturing, and growing. As I mentioned earlier, I use to think that once I got "there," wherever that place was, I would be happy and complete. I now know it is a process, an ever-changing journey, and that every day is truly a gift.

So I turn the painting now to an individual canvas rather than a wall or a room or a whole house. What are you working on? What colors are you choosing for your latest creation? Is your picture happy or sad? Is it a self-portrait or an abstract? Is it detailed or random? There is no correct answer for everyone, as we are all different.

What matters most is that you are exploring and experimenting. Keep your brush moving. Pause to reflect and admire your work. There is always another blank canvas. Expect touch-ups as you create. Relax, no mistakes are ever truly made—they are only lessons to learn along the way.

Let food be thy medicine,
and medicine be thy food.
—Hippocrates

chapter 5
Food and Mood

Ancient medicine uses food to heal and promote wellness. There are foods that can inhibit and foods that can enhance, foods that can heal or destroy.

For our purpose here, this book will focus on a tiny little sliver of the food world, but one that has changed my life and possibly can change yours too. Most likely if you are reading this book, you are open-minded. You are probably familiar with emotional eating. You might have done it, still do it, or know someone who does.

Think of a time when you were truly happy in your life—a time when you were carefree. Now think about what your diet was like at that time. I am guessing it might be harder to remember specifics of what you were eating on a day-to-day basis and you remember more details of your favorite song, an outfit you looked amazing in, or perhaps meeting the love of your life. Food was part of that time, but not so memorable.

Now fast forward, or if you are lucky enough to rewind here, think of a time when you weren't so happy—when things in your life might have been rocky or uncertain. For some of us, we might have been overweight, finding our only joy in what we call "comfort foods." These are foods that we got pleasure from when we ate them, smelled them, or cooked them. Like music, food can elicit many memories from our past, both good and bad.

I want to share some thoughts on the power of food and how it can relate to you being your best. Most of us are more particular about the car we drive, the designer purse we carry, or the coffee we drink than the food we buy and put into our bodies. If you have ever had food poisoning, you have a moment when you pray that if and when you feel better you will never take a chance on eating something bad again. You are so happy to be better that you are cautious, very cautious, at least for a while, until life takes over and you fall back into your old routine. However, many foods can act like poison in our bodies.

Do you know that many of the aches and pains, illnesses, and inconsistent energy levels you experience on a regular basis are impacted by the foods you eat? You might be thinking this is a crazy statement, or that yes, you believe it, but it does not apply to you. I have spent the past eight years studying and experimenting with food. In my own personal experience and research, it never fails to fascinate me. My daughter Kelsey has had many sensitivities to food. No absolute life threatening allergies but definitely sensitivities. We finally sought out the evaluation and opinion of a functional medicine doctor to get to the bottom of things. A functional medicine doctor has a much more comprehensive holistic approach than a typical conventional Western medicine doctor. We were often recommended that she just take a pill to make the symptom go away. It is amazing how your body screams, even shouts back at you when something doesn't agree with it. We are often too busy or unaware that the very food we consume can cause us so much upset and havoc within.

Visit my website, www.kelly-kurtz.com, to complete a complimentary health history assessment and learn more about how the foods you are eating are affecting you.

Finding Out What You Are Hungry For

Have you ever had a craving for something and you were trying to be "good" and not have that particular thing? Chances are that you ate just about everything else and in the end, you still ended up craving what you wanted in the first place.

You see, our bodies are amazing creatures. They know so much more than we give them credit for. The craving might be physiological or psychological or both. We might be lacking a particular mineral or vitamin and our bodies want a food that will supply that. We might be lonely and need to feel wanted, needed, or cared for, thus the need for comfort foods that can elicit those feelings for us.

Can you remember who you were before the world told you who you should be? —Unknown. Is food filling up your space and keeping your authentic self from showing its true colors?

As a health coach, while receiving my training at The Institute for Integrative Nutrition, I learned about a concept called primary foods. Surprisingly I also learned about a similar concept nearly 25 years ago while I was in school to become a registered occupational therapist. It was called work-life balance, and this is much of what the principles of occupational therapy are based on.

I think I have always believed in this concept and now I see it so clearly that it is in my every thought process daily. I ask myself questions, such as "How does this promote all that I want in my life? Does this serve me? Does it defeat me? Am I going toward balance or drifting away?" Although I am trying to live in the present moment, it might sound like this is a lot of work to be answering these questions on the drop of a dime. But as they become second nature, they will help define your goals and dreams.

As part of my health coaching services, I can and will explore this concept with you. We will look at your "circle of life" and define and seek balance for you individually. As we are all unique, what works for you just might not work for me. It is your blueprint, your puzzle, and your mosaic pattern. Visit my website, www.kelly-kurtz.com, at any time during this book to get started.

I know, for me, when I am out of balance, I seek different things. After years of self-destructive behaviors, I know my patterns fairly well. I am somewhat predictable in many ways. I used to beat myself up and my inner voice would be "angry" or "laughing cynically" at me saying, "Here you go again, Kelly." Now I can identify the pattern as it is beginning or in the early stages of repeating. Sometimes I can even stop it before it starts.

One story I have heard is about a woman who walks to work the same way every day. One day she steps in a hole and rolls her ankle, the next day she breaks the heel on her shoe, another day she scrapes the toe of her shoe, and some days it's a tiny stumble, but every day she steps in the same hole. She knows it's there yet she does it every day. She has come to expect it and believes it is her destiny to step in it. Then one day her ankle is really sore. It is swollen and bruised and she has had just about more than she can take. She decides to try something different, slightly deviant and tricky. Today something is different; she anticipates the hole from several feet back. As she approaches it she purposefully steps over it, she laughs, she smiles, and she says "not today."

What are you craving or longing for in your life? Do you need love? Compassion? Greater faith? How about a more fulfilling job or career? Are you seeking greater education? How is your health? Your home environment? Do you come home to an empty house day after day and an empty bed night after night? Do you have friends and meaningful relationships? How is your financial situation? Are you in debt and do not feel worthy of all you desire? These are some tough questions but ones that are basic to not only who you are but more importantly, who you believe you are and can and should be.

These are the kind of things we explore in health coaching. They are relatively simple questions with rather powerful answers. Are you ready to take your life to the next level? Take a moment to ponder and answer some of these questions.

_____

_____

_____

_____

_____

How many times do you find yourself eating crap? Do you want ice cream, rich chocolate cake, cookies, and pastries? Do you feel satisfied after you have had them, or do you feel good while eating them, then crappy afterward? Is it the act of eating these foods or the feeling you get from eating them?

In the past, I had many times when I felt like I wanted something and just could not put my finger on what it was. I tried many things. I would eat a pizza, bake a pan of brownies, or eat a dozen chocolate-chip cookies. Did I feel better? Maybe temporarily, but not ultimately. That is the stuff I am talking about. I think food is self-medicating, just like alcohol or an addiction to painkillers or something else. It consumes you for the feeling that you get, then it's gone, or at least the food is. The feelings might linger, intensify, or dissipate until they return. Sadness can be a lifestyle. "Depression hurts," as the commercial says. The quest for inner peace, self-love, and affection is powerful stuff. We all want it and yet a small handful of us actually have it.

I want you to think about what it is that you are seeking. What do you want and desire? Do you want to be healthy and fit? Do you try really hard one day, one week, or even longer, and then jump on the scale only to realize that you haven't lost any weight or so little that you feel your effort was a waste? Usually when that happens, the scale dictates your mood. It can instantly make you happy or sad. It can deflate you; a mere number can direct your entire day.

Years ago when I first began working with Jeff, my life coach, he told me to put the scale away. I admit I liked the thought of not knowing, not facing my demons daily or weekly. But it went against the grain of everything I had ever known about weight loss or dieting. I mean, who hasn't experienced the weekly weigh-in at Weight Watchers? You know, wearing the same outfit even down to the underwear so you can get the most accurate results of .2 pounds lost. Right? Well, at least you didn't gain. Then onward to another week until something crazy happens, such as you had a stressful week, or it was Halloween or the Easter candy was 75 percent off and you just had to finish off the last bag of Cadbury mini eggs so you wouldn't eat them anymore.

Putting away the scale was one of the most powerful lessons I learned. For the first time, I learned to trust myself and listen to my body. I stayed true to myself and to my mission of getting and staying healthy. I began keeping a food journal and actually wrote down what I really ate. I wasn't measuring and weighing things or recording points. Instead I was trying to eat sensibly and healthy and began switching to whole foods—foods that weren't entirely prepackaged, microwaved, boxed, bagged, or unwrapped.

I started to work out at the gym, wear slightly less baggy clothes, and even wear a little lip gloss. I updated my music play list and cleaned out my sad songs for some new ones. Changes began to happen—no, not overnight, but small changes. I started to feel better, different, and encouraged. I started to change. I think I was finally ready to take some action. The things I had previously been doing hadn't really gotten me where I wanted to be or go. I began to feel that I was in control of what I put in my mouth and in my body. I started to notice how different foods made me feel. For the first time in my life, I realized that food did not have to control me any longer.

I began shedding weight. How did I know, you ask, if I wasn't weighing myself? I could tell, people could tell. My clothes were fitting me differently, I started to feel different inside, and I even looked different on the outside. I started to feel excited, As if I had a secret that was waiting to burst from the inside out. I was beginning to feel happier. The progress I was making was really a transformation. No other word to call it than that— transformation. I was getting my groove back. I had a long road ahead, but the path was hikeable, manageable terrain, and I was up for the challenge!

During the next several months, I managed to lose more than forty pounds. I did finally get on the scale with the approval of my coach, but only after I had changed my mind set. You see, he knew that even if the number on the scale had been just ten pounds, it would have been amazing because of how I felt.

As I continued my journey, I decided to start my own home-based business in the health and wellness industry and become an independent distributor with a company called USANA health sciences, which manufactures pharmaceutical-grade nutritional supplements.

I had been taking these supplements for several months and I truly felt amazing. I wanted to learn more, so I could be a resource to other people. When you experience something like I am talking about, a whole body and mental shift, you simply cannot remain silent. You want to shout it from the rooftop and tell everyone you know, so they too can feel what you are feeling.

I was starting to see the bigger picture of how food is more than what we buy at the grocery store. It also involves the highest quality nutritional supplements, it involves what we put on our skin as health and beauty products, and it involves exercise. These are lifestyle puzzle pieces.

In just a few short months, once my business was gaining momentum, I wanted to further my education. I contacted the National Exercise and Sports Trainers Association (NESTA) and enrolled in a program to become a certified kid's nutrition specialist. I was a mom with real life experience. I knew nutrition was the key to having better health and increased energy. I knew that this was the connection that so many people needed. It was lifestyle that needed to change. Not just diet, not a quick fix, but a change in mind set, a belief in myself and that I was worthy of love and nurturing, that my body deserved love and nourishing foods. If I took pride in myself and in my appearance, if I believed I could, then I would. I wanted to help parents feed their children well, so they would develop healthy lifelong habits.

Things started to change for me. I began holding educational seminars and started helping families, particularly moms who were overwhelmed and overburdened. I knew that they wanted to feed their families healthy nutritious foods. I knew that they were crunched for time and looking for solutions. I had done with my family what many were looking to do with theirs, and I needed to share. I spoke to my kids' sports teams and their parents, along with their coaches. I was seeing firsthand the powerful effect that food had on performance and energy.

Eating Like a Champion

My son is a great athlete. He excels on and off the field. He is lean and fit and eats well. When he was in the eighth grade, he was playing his final year of American Youth Football (AYF). He had been playing with this group of boys since he was seven years old. Youth football has restrictions on age and weight to make a more level playing field and to maximize the players' safety. Every August 1, the official start of the season, the team mates would come out to begin the grueling conditioning camp.

One of the first things the boys were required to do was weigh-in. Kids needed to be within a weight range to qualify to play on a certain team. The weigh-in was crucial to see if they needed to move up to the next level or move down, depending where they fit in the guidelines. AYF would recognize the fact that these were boys and that they were growing, so there was an allowance for weight to increase incrementally as the season progressed.

Because it was the final year for many of the boys, they all wanted to finish together on the same team. Some were over the weight limit and felt that they could "starve" themselves and make it. As you can imagine this is a dangerous idea on many levels and strongly discouraged by the organization and the coaches.

I was a member of the board for our town's program, so I routinely was at practices, especially during the first few weeks during conditioning. I was assisting with recording the weights, so I saw the boys' expressions change when they stepped onto the scale. Some smiled, some were completely discouraged, and I even saw a few tears. They all desperately wanted to be part of this team.

At ages 10, 11, and 12, some were being told they were "too heavy" to play. I knew with my training from NESTA that I could be of assistance by offering some general education, helpful hints, and to serve as a resource to the boys and their parents.

I organized a seminar right there on the field one night after practice. I met with the team members. We discussed how they were working really hard in practice. I wanted to have them think about the importance of good nutrition. They were getting older and beginning to make a lot of their own food choices. I wanted to assist them with ensuring that they put the best possible "fuel in their bodies." We discussed how good quality food really mattered. They began to see that junk "in" meant junk "out" and that eating highly processed foods, loaded with chemicals and sugars, would end up leaving them depleted.

I offered suggestions and gave them some ideas to try. I gave them a handout they could take home and put on their refrigerators. They learned how to take responsibility to pack healthy snacks and lunches. They also took responsibility for the food they put in their bodies. They worked with their parents to make the best choices. It was amazing to see them gel as a team and take nutrition seriously.

Something amazing happened as a result of their desire and commitment to themselves and their teammates. I saw turkey roll-ups and apple slices replace donuts, sodas, and Twizzlers.

They were winning all right. They made it through regional competition all the way to the national championships in Orlando, Florida! Although they didn't capture the crown, the team was number two in the country that year. I truly believe that nutrition had a huge role in the success of the team. The boys started at the first of August and played through December without illness or injury. They all made weight week after week by making healthy choices and taking care of themselves. Diet, vitamins, and exercise were all key components to their success along with the desire to succeed.

The next summer another dream-come-true would happen for my son. His baseball team made it all the way to the Babe Ruth World Series in Murray, Utah. He was the starting pitcher in game one and was named the game's most valuable player (MVP). (OK, it is not essential that I tell you this detail, but I am so proud of him!) Before the trip to Utah, I spent time talking with the boys about their food choices.

We talked about how what they ate would impact how they felt and played. If they had salt, soda, and sugary drinks on the plane, it would leave them feeling bloated and tired. We discussed how eating highly processed food with little fiber and nutrients would leave them feeling constipated or off their routine.

These were tough conversations to have with 13-year-old boys. It was tough enough for a mother to have individually with her son, but I was talking to a whole team of teenage boys. They listened, they were interested, and they accepted the challenge. They wanted this championship, and they saw the power of choices and how it could impact their goals and outcomes.

What are you eating that slows you down and makes you feel sluggish, tired, and blah? What is your body trying to tell you about the fuel you are filling it up with? Listen carefully, as you just might be astonished at what you find.

Planting Your Garden—Eating the Rainbow

Healthy eating—that title or topic is everywhere you look, from the news to radio and television advertisements to magazine covers. It is the topic of articles, blogs, and books. We all strive to be healthy and want to do what is best for us most of the time. The difficult part is knowing what to believe, which advice to follow, and finding food that works for your body. We are all individual and we all have certain foods that make us feel good and energized and others that do not.

You might be bored with cooking and too tired to put a whole lot of energy into dinner, let alone three meals a day. Food is powerful stuff. It is essential and something we all have in common. We are busy people. We often want and need something quick, easy, and simple.

If your kids are grown, you likely can remember the days of packing their lunches. You might remember a favorite lunch box or a childhood food or snack. Not long ago, the threat of the famous "Twinkie" disappearing took over the news. Stories popped up in the news, people reminisced and consumers bought the remaining boxes off the shelves. Although many of us hadn't had one in years, the threat of not ever having one again made us sad—the end of an era, so to speak.

You see, food brings up feelings and memories for us all. Today's "food" is genetically engineered, genetically modified, and really just a few ingredients short of being plastic. How did this happen? How did we get here? The grocery stores are lined with boxes, bags, and pouches of all kinds of things. The packages are like billboards fighting for our attention. Brighter graphics, super slogans, and promises of low fat, more fiber, wholegrain, fortified, enriched, and just heat and serve!

When I first began my journey several years ago, I started to learn about the power of food and the effects it has on our moods and energy levels. As I began exploring and ultimately feeling better, it fueled me to go further into this journey. Now as a certified health coach, I help clients explore and experience this all the time. The profound realization that one human's passion is another human's poison is true. What works for you might not necessarily work for me.

Finding your "fuel" is truly empowering once it happens and your body begins to function as nature intended. YOU become a well-oiled machine! In order to do this, you have to start somewhere. Because we are all individuals, we all are a little different. I always like to go back to writing—journaling and really identifying where you are right now.

For this step, I recommend keeping a food diary for at least a few days to a week. Many of you have done something like this if you have ever been on Weight Watchers. This journal is different, because you are not weighing and measuring food or counting points. What you want to do is write down what you eat, what time you eat it, how you are feeling just before you eat, how you feel afterward immediately, then how you feel thirty minutes and one hour later, and how long before you are hungry or eat again. It might sound like a lot of work, but believe me if you are truly interested in reclaiming your life you cannot ignore your food!

Once you begin to pay attention to this and how you feel, you can start to tweak your diet and your "fuel." Ask yourself questions, as the answers are before you. "I feel tired." OK, what did you just eat? Pasta, cookies, candy. "I have an upset stomach." OK, the last thing you ate was yogurt thirty minutes ago. "I feel bloated." OK, maybe eating the three-bean salad and apple and the bran muffin was too much fiber all at once.

You see your body is shouting at you but you are often too busy to hear what it is saying. As your health coach, I can assist you in figuring all this out. If you identify some triggers after you eat a certain type of food, pay careful attention when you eat it again. If you get the same or similar results, chances are you have sensitivity to that food. Eliminating one or two things at a time, then reintroducing them back one at a time, can help clue you in to this.

One rule of thumb that really is universal is to eat locally, seasonally, and fresh. By doing these three things you can pretty much guarantee you will feel better. I realize there are parts of the world where this isn't the case, but for you, the readers of my book, I believe it to be true. Find yourself a local farm that practices good farming and is pesticide free and organic, if at all possible. If that isn't possible start at your local grocery store.

Stay to the perimeter of the store, where you will find fresh vegetables, fruit, fish, meat, and dairy. Whether you are vegan or vegetarian, Paleo or eat a combination of food selections, the perimeter is really the way to go. The inner aisles contain prepackaged, boxed, bagged, and highly processed stuff. The majority of concoctions there aren't really food—they are chemical formulas.

Remember that what you put into your body has a big role in what you get out of your body in terms of your health. Locally grown foods are picked closer to when they are ripe versus being picked early and having to travel by boat, train, or plane to reach your grocery cart. Chances are locally grown foods are less expensive and fresher and you can feel good about supporting a community business as well.

Consider joining a community supported agriculture or farm share program where you can get fresh, local, in-season produce weekly. I have done this for the past few years and I love it. I don't have room at my condo for a garden, but I can get fresh delicious produce every week as if it was homegrown. Contact your local chamber of commerce or health food store to find one near you.

Another area of food that I find interesting is Ayurvedic medicine. Did you know that if you are feeling scattered and frazzled, you might be craving root vegetables? Yes, carrots, sweet potatoes, and turnips can help to ground you.

Do you feel easily agitated, irritable, and overly competitive? Try reducing hot foods, spicy foods, and red meats in your diet. Add more cooling foods, such as fish or chicken. Increase your intake of sweet vegetables, such as squash, sweet potatoes, parsnips, or beets.

There is a lot to be learned from Chinese medicine. One of the most interesting concepts that I have studied and found simply fascinating is the Five Element Theory. It is based on the premise that you must create harmonious meals that help keep you grounded and balanced.

Foods are placed into categories or elements of the Earth and include wood, fire, soil, metal, and water. I encourage you to experiment with your food to see how it impacts your mood. Get your journal and make some notes. You more than likely will be amazed by what you will discover about yourself and the correlation to what you eat and how you feel.

Although I am not an expert in Ayurvedic medicine by any means, I do see the power in it. As your health coach, together we can explore some of these options I have mentioned and others, so that you can truly use food to enhance and support your mood to one that is in alignment with your life's purpose.

As you apply the concepts of *Fresh Paint* to your life, think of all the great colors that good food has to offer. There is a rainbow of various colors in fresh fruits and vegetables that you won't find in boxed foods. Think of this as adding beautiful colors to the inside of your body to shine forth in better skin, hair, nails, and the brightness of your eyes and your smile.

Preventative Maintenance

Loving yourself is vital to being happy. You must believe you are worthy of being cared for. Your body is your haven, your castle, and your house. Without it, you have nothing. This quote really resonated with me: "Ignore your health and it will go away," because it's so true. Maybe not today and maybe not tomorrow but before you know it, it will happen.

You must care for yourself along your journey. As mothers and spouses, we have often neglected ourselves in return for caring for everyone else. For example, we put exercise last on the "to-do" list and feel that we are not worth taking the time to do anything special to nourish and nurture ourselves. We overextend ourselves with unnecessary commitments and then we're too tired to care.

We allow our appearances to relax, hoping no one will see us, thus the "People of Walmart" website and videos appear on the Internet. We laugh at these people, but do not become one of those women, because you deserve more.

You are beautiful and strong. How we feel on the inside is a direct correlation to how we look on the outside. So do you show up for work with clothes that look like you slept in them? Do you think no one will notice? They might seem like minor things, but in actuality, they are not. Value yourself enough to care.

Vitamins

There is a lot of talk in the news regarding vitamins. The mainstream society will tell you that you get everything you need in your food, after all it is, "fortified with vitamins and minerals," "calcium added," "fortified and enriched," "whole grain," and more. However, I will tell you that there is plenty of research that supports taking a high-quality, pharmaceutical grade, multivitamin supplement that is necessary and essential to good long-term health. It is a piece of the puzzle in which the combination of eating the highest quality food you can afford, getting regular exercise, and taking your vitamins is essential each and every day.

There is no way we can get all we need from our food. No one eats perfectly each and every day, 365 days a year. What fun would that be? Eating healthy most days, exercising regularly, and taking good vitamins gives you the best shot at staying healthy and maintaining a good strong immune system.

Visit my website www.kelly-kurtz.com

You can't direct the wind,
but you can always adjust your sail.
—A Proverb

chapter 6
The Art of Home Staging

Let me share a story of how I got from where I was to where I am. Hang in there and it will all make sense. I remember when I was engaged to be married and my fiancé and I were looking to buy our first house. We would drive through neighborhoods and pick out our favorites. Some were way out of our price tag and we deemed them the "someday" house. We looked at others that were moderate and cute and then some that had been abandoned but had potential for sure.

Although I really liked the idea of owning a "someday house," we were rational. I was just 23, a college graduate, and a new professional. I was a registered occupational therapist, and he was a mechanical engineer, both well paid and in demand. We were young, just starting out, and wanted to be financially smart. We began looking at two-family houses with the hope of living in one part and renting the other to help us with our mortgage.

We looked at many places. Some were completely dumpy, wires running amuck, plumbing that needed replacing, and musty basements that made a skunk smell sweet. We searched and searched and then we happened on a pretty little Dutch colonial that had just been freshly painted a pretty shade of yellow with crisp white trim and classic black shutters. We immediately got excited as we pulled up to the house.

I think I already wanted to buy it and I hadn't even gotten out of the car yet. We went inside and, yes, it was love at first sight. The owners were there, which wasn't usually the case in the other houses we had seen with our Realtor (who happened to be my best friend's mother). The house was warm and inviting. It was bright and cheery. It was perfect for us. The basement didn't smell and it even had a built-in cedar closet!

We went upstairs to tour the apartment that would serve as our rental unit, and although it wasn't quite as nice as the owner's unit, it was cute and had a lot of true potential. I remember the butterflies in my belly and the excitement of "Oh, my god, I am going to have a house!" We made an offer the next day and my mind began thinking about decorating! I was picturing what would go where or what type of furniture we could buy.

The wedding was still several months away, but the planning began and that moment really planted the seed of the love of decorating in my soul. As the next few months passed, we were busy with wedding planning, work, and preparing to move into our new house.

I can remember the feelings of move-in day—walking into our new house for the first time. The empty house was like a blank canvas—open to so many possibilities. It was so much fun to unpack and put away all our wedding gifts—new dishes, silverware, linens, and more. It felt fresh and clean and ours.

I will never forget that first home. It was a place where a lot of transition happened. It was going from college to getting engaged and planning a wedding, and then, at 23, with a new house and a new husband.

I spent time getting creative. I borrowed my mother's sewing machine and made simple curtains for my dining room and living room. I signed up for a flower-arranging class and began making dried arrangements, wreaths, and swags. I learned how to cook more than Ramen noodles, frozen veggies, and bagels, which had essentially gotten me through four years of college.

Although it was a time of transition, it was also a time of self-discovery. A few years passed and we found ourselves busy with graduate school, and a remodel of the upstairs apartment. We were yearning for something more, we began taking rides again on the weekend driving through various neighborhoods and once again looking at the "someday houses." This time they were bigger and better, as building in our area had taken a surge. The neighborhoods of beautiful colonial houses with lush lawns and two- and three-car garages, along with two-story foyers and vaulted ceilings began to entice us.

We thought we would "just look" at a few "open houses" and that is all it took. We wanted to be in a bigger and newer house, one that could accommodate friends and family and would offer us room to grow. We found many options, went through the numbers, and were in the process of making an offer when we discovered an amazing house that we learned was just becoming available. It was in the town we had grown up in and just a mile from my parents.

This house was huge—more than 2,500 square feet. It was custom everything, had huge curb appeal, crazy amazing bathrooms, and an incredible kitchen. The hardwood floors were to die for. I felt compelled. I wanted it. I needed it. I had to have it! We bantered back and forth for a few weeks until finally it was ours.

The house we were currently living in would fit in its entirety in about two rooms of this new one. The walls were all crisp white, the natural light was stunning, and completely empty this house was truly magnificent! Once again, I couldn't sleep. I had visions of decorating. I plowed through magazine after magazine looking for ideas. Yet again, I was excited beyond belief at the possibility of this house.

The view out the back windows was nothing short of spectacular. The sunrise over the hills was like being on a permanent vacation, and I thought at that moment I would never move again. I was at my destination at 25 years old and had all that I desired. The next year was filled with fun, finishing up my MBA, spending time with my mother antiquing, and finding treasures for my amazing house.

Our first child, Connor, was born and nearly two years later our daughter, Kelsey, came along. We were complete—great jobs, master's degrees, two amazing children, and my parents close by. Life was good and I was the luckiest person in the world. We spent 10 years in that home and everyone who knew we lived there commented on what a lovely house we had. How they had admired it and thought it was simply beautiful.

Then one day I was driving to the center of town on an errand and something caught my eye—a cute little mint green cottage that I had always liked as a kid. The people who lived there always had it decorated so nicely. There was a tree out front that they would hang colored Easter eggs on in the spring and it always looked so charming, like a doll house.

As I drove by, I noticed that there was a "for sale" sign on the front lawn. I remember saying out loud, "oh my, I must go inside." I went home and called the listing agent. I left a message and waited for a return call. Several hours later, the return call came and the next day I was pulling into the driveway of the mint green cottage for my personal showing.

I know this might sound crazy, but I guess the wow of the huge colonial had worn off. I hadn't really realized it until then. It was 10 rooms to clean, a huge yard with tons of leaves to rake, grass to mow, bark mulch to spread, gardens to tend to, and weeds to pick. The kids were busy with school and sports and it consumed our weekends. It was perfect inside and outside, but it was consuming a lot of time and energy.

We had a beautiful place, truly we did. Somehow even though I was in my "someday house" I found myself yearning for something more. This little house up the street was simple, it had charm and character. It was mint green, for Pete's sake, it needed a makeover! I wanted it, I needed it, and I was drawn to it. I remember being out on its rustic screened-in porch and I called my husband and said, "You just have to come see this, it is adorable." And so he did.

After a few days of discussion and multiple revisits, we decided to make an offer. Now everyone I knew was wondering what the heck was wrong? Were we bankrupt and had to sell the big house? Were we just plain crazy? Who in their right mind would trade what we had for what we now wanted?

The process of evolving is amazing to me. You can see from my story during the past few pages, that I evolved. It seems to happen without notice, slowly at first, then all at once— it's you. It is kind of like when your children are small, and you have a family celebration with folks you might not have seen for a while. They always seem to comment on how "big the kids have gotten."

It's true we do not often see the little day-to-day changes, but rather when a bigger picture or more significant change appears. Small simple changes, small daily actions can add up to big results. That is what I am referring to here. Change and growth are good. Staying stagnant never really has worked for me. I like consistency and routine, but change is good.

The new "old" house needed work, lots of work—plumbing, electrical, heating, flooring updates and refinishing, and of course paint and wallpaper. I started a notebook with ideas, color samples, and names and numbers of contractors to contact. I became excited again at the possibility of a new project, saving a diamond in the rough, making it shine again. Slowly new life began to flow into this moderate-sized cottage and it became a warm and comfortable new place to call home.

> *When you walk into your home at the end of a grueling day, do the stresses and strains fall away, or does the clutter and disharmony add further to your headaches? Is your home the nurturing haven it should be, or is it a continuation of the chaos of the outside world?*
>
> —Beverly Pagram

If you could describe your home with one word or phrase, what would it be? Serenity and love? Relaxed and comfortable? Cheerful and serene? Shabby-chic? Cool and sleek? Streamlined and simple?

Take a few moments and think about your home. Does it call to you? Does being there make you feel restful, peaceful, and content? Or are you stressed out and overburdened with clutter, unfinished projects, broken furniture, or overgrown shrubbery? Whatever it is, you are not alone. There are always projects to do, things on our wish list and to do lists, which for a variety of reasons never get done. That is life sometimes. We must prioritize our time and financial resources and most of us don't feel good about going into debt just so we can have a granite counter top.

Can a Towel Change Your Life?

I am going to share with you a bit about the concept of home staging. This is a service that homeowners can use or that Realtors recommend when they are trying to sell a property. A good example of this is often called the "model home." If you have ever viewed a "model home" you know what I am referring to. Everything is beautiful, perfect, and in place. There is no clutter, no stained furniture, no cabinets and junk drawers that won't close because there is too much stuff in them. The closets aren't jammed with stuff you never wear, are they? No, they usually display beautiful items all perfectly aligned with not a wrinkle in sight and all evenly spaced just right. Now for me, being a bit on the obsessive-compulsive side, this kind of stuff inspired and excited me. I love that kind of simplicity and organization, but in reality, who really can live like that?

I am here to tell you that you can have your own version of the model home. Think back to the dream board we talked about in Chapter 2. Do you have any pictures of a room or house that you can relate to? I am going to break the next few sections into rooms to make it easier for you to chunk and not make you feel overwhelmed. This should be fun, it should be exciting, and will allow you to express yourself creatively. I realize you might have a spouse, a significant other, or children who live with you that you have to consider. You can share ideas and incorporate the creativity of everyone.

The Bloom Room: Just Add Water

You can start small. Maybe begin with your bathroom. This can be a crazy place, especially if multiple people are using it. The bathroom is often overlooked as a place to find peace and serenity because many people are rushed when they are in there, always running late for work or for an appointment, brushing your teeth while applying your mascara, or putting in your earrings.

What if you look at your bathroom in a different light? Right now, go look. Look through the eyes of a potential homebuyer, what do you see? Are there dried-up globs of toothpaste in the sink? Is the toilet paper roll empty and bare? How about a maze of electric cords dangling off the counter from various appliances used on your hair? Is the mirror spattered with hairspray? Is this the look you are going for? No, I am guessing not. But I realize if it is a choice between being late for your meeting or making Martha Stewart proud, you will take the former.

I want to propose that you reconsider the bathroom to be an important place and therefore you treat it like one. The bathroom is a place where lots of self-care happens. You care for your body there. Your shower is vital in cleaning and refreshing your wonderful self. Take a look at what's in your shower. Do you have multiple shampoo bottles, body washes, body scrubs, and razors lining the edges? What kind of products do you buy? Are they loaded with chemicals that you need a PhD in chemistry to decipher?

I am asking you to simplify. Reduce the clutter. Try an over-the-shower organizer to display the products you have selected for cleaning your amazing body. Most of us take more time picking out the air freshener scent for our car than we do selecting a nourishing shampoo, body wash, and conditioner for ourselves.

The shower should be a time of celebration that you are healthy and taking care of your body. When you get out of the shower, what kind of towels do you have? Are they the ones you have had for 15 years that are all frayed and paper thin? If you have ever had the pleasure of going to an upscale hotel, you likely remember the towels and perhaps the bathrobe (plush, soft, luxurious) that was in the bathroom.

Once again, I bring up my favorite store, TJMaxx, where there are these kinds of upscale bath items at great discount prices. Can a towel change your day, your mind set? You might think I am crazy, but I say, "Yes, it can!" The morning ritual of taking a shower with lovely citrus-scented shampoo and body wash followed by wrapping yourself in a soft luxurious towel says, "Yes, I am worth it!"

How about a pretty basket or container to keep your after-shower products? They can be displayed, if you have space, or tucked neatly under the sink. It is again soothing to pull out your supplies that are neat and organized as opposed to fishing them out day after day among a pile of stuff under the sink.

Look at what's under your sink. Can you toss half-used bottles and unwanted products that have expired or that you no longer use? Clearing out the space makes room for tranquility and will reduce the stress you feel while getting ready in the morning. Try this! You will be amazed at what this simple cleanse can do for you.

The Orange Crush

Following my divorce I put a down payment on a condo, I was thrilled at the thought of moving into my first real place! I spent a lot of time planning and preparing. I truly used visualization techniques and the power of intention. And yes, Pinterest too! I had time so I began thinking about my space as a coat of Fresh Paint. I knew I wanted something different in this home. I wanted some familiar touches and comforts, but I knew this was a clean start.

It needed to feel different from anything I had lived in before. I was drawn to the feeling of a simple life—one of carefree comfort. I wanted to use simple items that were functional and practical. I wanted my new home to be a retreat, a place where I could restore and reclaim my authentic self. I now saw things differently and the rehabbing I had done at my dad's house was essential for me to be at this point now.

This next phase was for redesigning. Redesigning the life I had imagined for so long with all the daydreaming I had done on my bike, and the times I had felt trapped and caged in an unhappy relationship that left me longing for something more. For years, I had thought I was destined to continue to be unfulfilled on many levels. The personal repurposing and restoring I had done had only gotten me so far.

For it was now, this moment that I was taking a leap of faith to have my own four walls that would be a place for peace, tranquility, and serenity. Three basic things that I had longed for were finally going to be possible. I began planning my rooms. I started browsing the furniture stores, looking for something that would inspire me and ignite my excitement and creativity.

I searched for weeks at every furniture store within a 50-mile radius.

Then one Saturday I was out once again searching. I turned the corner and there it was—a thing of beauty. It was a clean, almost contemporary, sectional sofa with a chaise longue on one end. It stopped me in my tracks and I knew I had found it. You are probably thinking every furniture store in America has a sectional like I am describing. Maybe, but this one was different. It was available in the most beautiful shade of orange—not burnt orange or rust, but primary orange—pure, clean, and fresh.

It was special ordered that evening. How bold was I to choose an orange sectional? The voice in my head had been jumping up and down trying to get my attention, but I said, "No, not now. This is my decision, not yours!" and wow, did that feel nice. As I proceeded through the store, I asked my sales person to show me anything she had in lime green for an accent chair. We looked at all kinds of styles, shapes, and sizes. Nothing was hitting me. Then she said, "OK, I have just one more for you to look at."

We took the elevator up to the fifth floor and as the door opened, my heart skipped a beat. Sitting there in the natural sunlight was the softest, sleekest, apple green, stress-less recliner with matching ottoman. The color had been discontinued and this was the only one available. The price tag was $1,788. Holy crap, that was more money than my first car.

My heart was racing as I sunk into its buttery soft leather—pure luxury. As I reclined and put my feet up, I imagined myself reading or sipping on a beverage in this chair. I imagined the feeling I would have from owning a piece of furniture (now two) that I truly loved. The kids were essentially grown. There would be no chocolate milk or juice box spills to stain this chair. It would be mine. I shocked myself again when before I could second-guess myself, I said in a loud and certain voice, "I'll take it."

I felt like a millionaire, like a big-shot executive making decisions in my own life. I can honestly say that was some empowering stuff. That moment, buying that furniture, was exhilarating. For the first time in my life, I was making a decision based on what I wanted. I didn't have to get permission, check, double check, or ask people for their opinions. Can you think of a time when you have had a similar experience? How did it make you feel?

_____

_____

_____

_____

_____

Who Are You Sleeping With?

Next, we move to the bedroom. The bedroom is a magical place for many reasons. In many ways, it too can define your day, your mood, and your overall outlook on life. Again, pretend you are the Realtor showing the master bedroom to potential buyers. As you approach the doorway, what is the first thing you see? What's your first impression of this space? Is there a pile of dirty clothing on the floor? Is the bed unmade? How about the dresser—is it piled with papers, clean laundry waiting to be put away, or enough loose change to empty a gumball machine? Make note of these impressions.

_____

_____

_____

_____

_____

If you are married or in a relationship, how is your love life? Is there still a spark between you? Is your bed a place of joy and passion and love? I don't mean that every day is like a honeymoon, but in general do you feel these emotions when you are there? Do you sleep well and wake up rested most of the time? If not, why? What wakes you or keeps you from sleeping at night?

Many times, we have fallen into routines that drain our energy. Televisions in the bedroom can be one of the biggest reasons we don't sleep well. Many people fall asleep to the television every night. I have never been a fan of having a TV in the bedroom. Lack of good quality sleep affects us in many ways. From headaches and irritability, difficulty thinking and learning, to a loss of sex drive, to name just a few. Other issues from loss of good quality sleep might include health problems, such as heart disease, high blood pressure, and stroke.

So what can you do to sleep better? I find this to be a common problem among the clients I coach. When we discuss this in our sessions, I often offer these suggestions as starting points to try. First, look at your bedtime routine. Often times, there is a lack of one and that is part of the problem. If you don't have a routine, let's work on establishing one. I realize that things come up and life happens, however, it is what you do most of the time that counts and establishes your healthy habits.

Here are some things to try. Pick one or two that resonate with you. Integrating these will likely allow you to start small and make true lifestyle changes, and you are more likely to stick with it.

- Pick a consistent bedtime within 15–30 minutes of the same time each night.

- 🕯 Begin turning off all electronic devices 30 minutes before you retire. This means cell phones, TV, laptops, iPads, et cetera.

- 🕯 Establish a night-time bathroom ritual of brushing and flossing or maybe applying a moisturizer to face, body, feet, and hands. How about a simple lip moisturizer or perhaps a dab of a calming essential oil, such as lavender, to your wrists, or the soles of your feet?

- 🕯 Try writing in a gratitude journal or adding to your gratitude jar that we discussed in Chapter 2.

Write down any last-minute thoughts that might keep you awake, such as something, you want to do tomorrow or that you forgot to do today. Writing them down releases them from taking space in your mind and therefore might allow you to sleep more peacefully and create space to dream!

I want to talk a bit about the physical space here, because it is important. Your bedroom should be peaceful and restful. It should be a retreat from the day and a place to rejuvenate and recover. Many basic cellular changes happen in our bodies while we sleep.

Look at your bed, your pillows, your sheets, and blankets. Do they call to you? Are they comfortable, soft, and inviting? If you have ever felt the difference between 250-count sheets and 600–800 count sheets, you know what I am referring too. Yes, the difference in price can be significant, but aren't you worth it? You don't need to have 10 sets of linen. One or two will do.

Make your bed special—warm and cozy in the colder months and cool and soothing in the spring and summer. Choose colors that call to you, relax you, and create the space you have imagined on your dream board or in your mind. Does it promote intimacy and peace? If you are still searching for your soul mate, does your bedroom reflect who and what you are looking for? Remember the movie *Field of Dreams* and the saying, "If you build it, he will come"? Well, this is one of those things. If you don't have that special someone in your life right now, work toward getting ready. They are out there and you are telling the universe that you are ready to receive them.

Since my marriage ended, I have done a lot of soul searching in many areas of my life. Love, passion, and romance have definitely been on my list of desires. For years, I slept in sweat pants, flannel pajamas, and big comfy clothing. I have been called toward pretty nightgowns with matching robes that are silky, soft, and sexy. For a long time, I just looked at them when I was out shopping, touching them and imagining the type of woman who would wear them, thinking about the love life she must have. How she and her partner must have a wonderful level of intimacy together.

Then one day I was looking for some new bras, and a beautiful deep rich purple robe caught my attention. I walked over to it to touch it and admire its soft silky texture. It felt rich and sexy in my hand. It was a set with a coordinating nightgown that had spaghetti straps and a sexy neckline that was different from the oversized "Life Is Good" T-shirt I routinely wore. I looked at the price tag, $24.99 for the set! Wow. I was worth $24. 99! I put it in my cart. For years, purchasing such an item would never have occurred to me. I was just fine in my comfy sweats; I was safe in them.

But this time, at this moment, something was different inside me, like the growth spurt of one of my children; it had been a gradual shift inside me. I felt joyful, excited, and happy about my new item I was about to purchase. No, there was nobody in my life yet, but I said to myself. "I deserve to feel this way. I don't need a man to wear this for. I am wearing it for me. I want to feel sexy again."

Loving yourself is so important. It goes back to living in the present moment. Using the good china and treating yourself like the amazing person you are. What are you wearing to bed? Who are you sleeping with? Don't wait. Imagine you are already there. What does that look like? What does it feel like? Waiting for a spark? Create it now. You have the power to ignite it!

The Pantry Purge

We cannot talk about renovations without talking about the kitchen! If you have ever watched the home-makeover shows on HGTV, you know I am not lying when I say that updating the kitchen will bring you a large return on investment. What

I am going to refer to here isn't to gut your kitchen back to the studs and spend $70,000 on an upgrade. If you are planning it and you have the budget, then good for you—how exciting!

For most of us, a simple pantry purge is in order and can make a tremendous difference in our lives without costing a lot of money. I am talking about some basic supplies, a well-stocked pantry, and a clutter-free work zone. Sound good?

As part of my health and lifestyle coaching, I offer this service to my clients. I have gone into their homes and assisted with clearing the clutter, getting them organized, providing sample menus, and even gone grocery shopping with some to help teach them to make simple but powerful lifestyle changes. Visit my website, www.kelly-kurtz.com, to find out how I can help you, either in person, by phone, by Skype, or other communication.

For now, let's talk about you, your kitchen, and where to begin. Now, I am guessing you want to eat healthy. Maybe you want to cook and prepare foods for yourself, you and your spouse or partner, or maybe even your entire family. This doesn't have to be difficult, but it does take some planning. Organization is the key ingredient to success. Are you not a very organized person? Don't worry, I can help. First, stand in your kitchen. Look around. Put your Realtor hat on and look long and hard. What is your first impression? Are the counters cluttered? Are there piles of bills, papers, and junk all around? If so, think how you feel when you look at it. Do you feel stressed or anxious?

Does your kitchen space look conducive to planning, prepping, and preparing healthy meals there?

Now go ahead, open up a cabinet. Does Tupperware come tumbling down and fall out? Can you see and find what it is you are looking for? How about your dishes? Are they chipped, cracked, and a mish mash of shapes and sizes? How about your pantry? What kinds of food are stored there? Cans, boxes, and bags? Do you have old or expired food? Are there cereal and cracker boxes that did not get closed properly and are now stale?

I have found that being organized in my kitchen is essential, because it's the most important room in my house. If my kitchen is well stocked and organized, then I am able to plan and prepare healthy food. Having good food ready allows me to eat healthy foods and therefore reduces waste, saves time, and money.

One of the services that I offer to my coaching clients is called the "Sunday Stock and Prep." I teach them how to identify what they want to eat, how to shop, and then bring it all home and begin preparing for the week ahead. The feedback has been amazing. Once you get into a routine, it truly makes life so much easier. I work with people who often eat take out three to five times a week, because they are simply "too busy" to go to the grocery store. I question "busy," as there seemed to be plenty of time for social events, TV shows, and leisure activities.

It is one thing to choose this lifestyle for yourself, but if and when you are responsible for feeding and nourishing your children, I find this sad that you don't choose to take good care of them. Perhaps this will be the subject of my next book—*Feeding the Healthy Family.*

For now, let's get back to business. I recommend stocking your kitchen with clear glass containers with plastic lids. I prefer glass over plastic, because it is safer and I discourage the use of plastic containers in general. Yes, sometimes they are convenient and even necessary. Do yourself a favor. Go and get a trash bag and go to that cabinet right now and take all your butter containers, plastic tubs, and miscellaneous cartons and toss them. Invest in a good set of containers with lids. Choose the ones that stack nicely, have the same covers, and are good quality food storage plastic.

Reusing previous food containers is not a great idea. You can use them to put screws, nails, or whatever, but don't reuse them for food. Many people reuse them, freeze in them wash them in the dishwasher, and reuse. The problem is these items weren't designed to be your storage containers. The plastic breaks down and the chemicals can leach into your foods and in turn into your body. This is also the same thing that microwaving in plastic does. I cringe in the lunchroom at work when people microwave in Styrofoam or plastic.

If you spend any money in your kitchen, invest in a set of various sizes of glass baking bowls and dishes. Pyrex makes a set that comes with a few rectangle casseroles and some round bowls. The set comes with lids and stack nicely in your cabinet or pantry. The thing I like about these is that you can see through them so you can identify what's in them. They fit well in your fridge, so when you are prepping your food for the week your refrigerator will look neat and organized. And the container that says "yogurt" actually contains yogurt.

I remember when I was transitioning to eating healthier. I had good intentions and I would do fairly well at the grocery store. The problem was once I got home I would load it all into the fridge. I was leaving out the prepping stage. I had every good intention of doing it later, really I did. However, Sunday night turned to Monday, and Monday turned to Tuesday, and then the sports schedule got hectic and the week got ahead of me and before I knew it, I was throwing out food week after week.

I once left a watermelon in the back of my refrigerator for a few weeks because I just didn't feel like cutting it up. When I finally got to it, it was all rotten inside—the smell was nasty and what a waste. Now I bring my groceries in the house and I leave all my produce out on the counter and prep it right away. I have my glass containers ready and I just do it.

Veggies are washed and cut. Chicken is baked, broiled, or grilled and put in a glass container for the week. Salad greens are rinsed and ready. Fruit is cut up and portioned into small containers of snack-size baggies to add to the lunch boxes in the morning.

I also went to the grocery store with a list of what I needed and had planned what was for meals for the week, so that I knew what I needed to buy. I'm sure that some of you are thinking that this sounds good, but really? You can't imagine knowing what you will eat for meals all week, let alone tonight. I am telling you, it is possible, even for you. Once you get organized and set your intention to do so, the tips and tools I am teaching you will help you to achieve this. Once it happens, you will wonder how you ever did it otherwise.

Now, because food and menus will vary greatly from person to person, I chose not to tell you what to buy or cook, that depends on what you like and what is good for your body. But some of the basic tools I believe everyone should have include.

- Insulated lunch box/bag or Bento lunch container
- Reusable ice packs
- Stainless steel, glass, or BPA-free plastic bottles (two)
- Clear glass containers for food storage, with plastic or glass lids to store in refrigerator
- Smaller size glass containers with plastic lids to bring in lunch box or plastic Rubbermaid containers to transport food
- Ziploc baggies, snack size and sandwich size, or reusable fabric pouches

Everyone will benefit from drinking more water. A good rule of thumb throughout the nutrition and fitness industry is to try to drink half your weight in ounces. So if you weigh 130 pounds, you should aim for 65 ounces of water daily. The best way to do this is plan for it. Most people have good intentions to drink water and often times the day gets ahead of them. You run into a meeting and didn't have a chance to grab a bottle from the vending machine, or you have been meaning to get to the break room to get some, but the phone hasn't stopped all morning.

By preparing and planning, you can change this scenario. By owning two good-sized water bottles (as mentioned above), you can calculate the amount of water you should have. Start your day with your two filled bottles that you take to work with you. This way they are ready. You can sip on it during your commute. You can have a bottle with you on your desk, so you can sip on it throughout the morning. Did you know that a glass of water first thing in the morning, before you have anything else, even your coffee, can give you a great boost, aid in digestion, and energize you?

Having consistent bottles can be beneficial in that you can take them with you wherever you go. So many people drink extra coffee, because there is usually a pot at the office and it is easy to grab a cup or two. Having your water with you at all times will allow you to sip on it throughout the day, stay hydrated, and mentally clear and sharp. There is no need to track how many disposable bottles you drank or spend lots of money on cases of water. Invest in a great, fun, funky bottle, and you will be surprised how much more you drink!

Adding the juice of a fresh lemon is a refreshing way to do this daily and a great way to start your day. Try drinking a mug of warm water with the juice of a freshly squeezed lemon before you have your coffee or tea in the morning. Lemon juice has many powerful benefits, including aiding in digestion and balancing your pH levels. Lemon juice can also strengthen your liver and help reduce inflammation in your joints by dissolving uric acid, which can build up and cause pain (see foodmatters.tv).

I am my own experiment.
I am my own work of art.
—Madonna

chapter 7
Exterior Work: Adding Curb Appeal

Let's talk about keeping your house safe. We have been discussing you and the feeling that your home and personal space have. I would like to talk about something else that is important to your health and well-being. It is about toxicity in your house. An amazing book, *The Healthy Home,* came out in 2011 and topped the *New York Times* bestseller list. It was written by Dr. Myron Wentz and by his son, Dave Wentz. The book is filled with information about hidden dangers and toxins in everyday products, from skin care to body care to cleaning products and even the dangers of the mercury amalgam fillings that many people still have in their mouths. Dr. Wentz is the Founder of USANA Health Sciences, the nutritional supplements company I mentioned earlier. (You can find out more about the nutritional products they offer through my website, www.kelly-kurtz.com.)

The information that Dr. Wentz shares in his book was really transformational to me. When I moved into my condo, I decided that I would only use natural cleaning products. This means you will not find chemical sprays and bottles or toxic cleaners under my sinks. Instead, you will find a gallon of white vinegar under each of my bathroom and kitchen sinks for cleaning the toilets, sinks, and tubs.

I use eco-friendly dishwasher tablets, dye-free and fragrance-free laundry detergent, and I even ditched my dryer sheets after reading this book. The smell of fresh laundry is really no smell at all. We have come to think that "clean and fresh" is the scent of the leading brand. It is actually chemicals, perfumes, and artificial scents. Those fragrances cling to the clothing and can be absorbed into your body. Imagine the effects of that day after day, week after week, and year after year. I encourage you to think about what that could mean in terms of endocrine and thyroid heath and cancers. The ingredients in these products are harmful or fatal if swallowed, but what about when they are absorbed into your body? It's like a nicotine patch that people use to stop smoking. Simply put it on your skin and the medicine is absorbed.

I was made aware that the detergents we put in our dishwashers are toxic, harmful, even fatal, if swallowed, and yet we eat and drink off the same dishes they were cleaned in. Trying to tackle everything at once is overwhelming. I encourage you to start simple. Pick up a copy of *The Healthy Home.* As you begin to run out of various products, try using white vinegar versus commercial bathroom cleaning products. You can buy a gallon for a fraction of what one bottle of the toxic stuff costs. Try using it on your floors too. It will make them sparkle. I promised you that you would find your sparkle if you read my book. You had no idea it would be because of vinegar, now did you?

Saying Yes, Saying No

The word "No" is one of the first words we learn as a child. Our parents tell us "No" all the time. "Do not touch." "Do not do that!" "No." As we get to be a little older, our parents don't let us do things we want. They say no to this and that. As adults, we tell our selves "No" a lot too. No, we do not deserve this or that, and no you can't and no you shouldn't and no, no and no.

I want to relook at saying "Yes!" Yes has a lot of power. Yes can allow you to feel again. So many emotions are associated with yes. Yes can give you hope. Yes can excite you, ignite you, and inspire you. Believe in yes. If they are truly "No's," can they be "No, not now" instead of a permanent "No"?

Sometimes no is for our own good, in our best interest, and it can even be the turning point in your life. For example, saying

"No more" to a relationship that no longer serves you, saying "no" to just going through the motions of your life without feeling and creating what you truly want, desire, and deserve.

Think about where you are in your life right now. Do you say no? Where do you want to say yes, and how can you allow yourself more yes responses in your life? Take a moment now and identify what you are longing to say "yes" to.

_____

_____

_____

_____

_____

How would saying yes allow you to feel?

_____

_____

_____

_____

_____

What is it costing you not to say yes?

_____

_____

_____

_____

_____

Self-Care Versus Health Care

How much time do you spend taking care of yourself each day, each week, and each month? Self-care can and does include bathing, dressing, grooming, hygiene, nutrition, exercise, and, of course, a spiritual component either through a meditative practice or through a religious denomination that you believe in. Do you take your body and health for granted? Do you assume it will just be there for you whenever you need to call on it? Do you overload it with caffeine, alcohol, highly processed foods and constant chronic daily stress? "Quit worrying about your health and it will go away." That is a powerful quote.

Taking care of one's self is really the first step in self-love. Yet it can often be viewed as selfish. It can make you feel guilty that you are taking time for yourself instead of taking care of everybody else. Yes, I think that often mirrors the definition of being a mother. I think there is a balance that can be achieved where you can have both. I didn't do that often, but I wish I had felt less guilt and more joy and more love of myself to do so.

Think about when you are on an airplane and before takeoff the flight attendant is reviewing emergency procedures. She tells you that if you are traveling with a child and the pressure changes in the cabin that the oxygen masks will fall down in front of you. You are instructed to take care of your breath first, and then assist the child. If you can breathe, you can better assist them. Pretty basic, right? How many of us would give it to our children first and then take a breath when we were just on the brink of passing out? That is my point. If you have waited so long to take your breath, you might feel like you are coming up for air, gasping to breathe.

Taking care of the body that houses your soul and spirit is a serious job. It is one that should not be taken lightly. It is not selfish. You should be nourishing your body with good, clean, whole foods and pure filtered water, exercising to keep your muscles and bones strong, so that you can embrace and enjoy all that your life has to offer. You want to be at peace with yourself, so that you can enjoy all that is good and purposeful in your life and have minimal stress so that when life throws something at you, you can handle it without it being broken.

I was having dinner with a dear couple, Dr. Peter Rugg and his wife, Patricia. They walk the talk in regard to a healthy and holistic lifestyle. I was sharing my book ideas with them and we began talking about the joy of self-care. Patti talked about how recently she rediscovered the tub bath again. Her kids were all grown and out of the house. She had a bathroom upstairs that she used to bathe her children in. It had a big, claw foot tub.

One day she decided to take a bath instead of the daily quick shower she was so accustomed to. She took it in the evening, filled the tub with nice warm water, added some mineral salts, lit a few candles, and soaked. She used a cotton cloth to gently exfoliate her skin. Her description of her experience in the bath was soothing. She reported having the most amazing night's sleep following that bath.

We need to take time to care for our bodies, take time to relax and appreciate and nourish the wonderful body that houses our heart and spirit. As a coach, I spend time on this topic of self-care with my clients. We explore ways to incorporate this into life. Below is a sample list of some ideas about how you can get started.

- **Daily moisturizer**—Choose your skin care products carefully, as your skin is your largest organ and much like a sponge. What you put on your body is absorbed into your body. Look for products that are paraben free and contain SPF. I recommend the Sense line. See my website for specifics: www.kelly-kurtz.com.

- **Brush and floss**—Sounds pretty basic, right? How about mixing it up a bit and trying different all-natural toothpastes. They come in refreshing flavors, are gentle on your teeth, and ditch the fluoride.

- **Oil pulling**—The use of coconut oil is gaining popularity. Try swishing this creamy miracle in your mouth for 20 minutes for at least three times a week. Not sure you can commit? Think you can't do it? Try swishing while you are in the shower, blow drying your hair, or even preparing dinner! The time goes by fast and this process will leave your teeth sparkling and your gums strong and healthy. Oh, yeah, just do not spit the oil down your drain when you're finished, as it will resolidify. Dispose of the oil in a container or your waste basket.

- **Tub bath versus shower**—Take a half-hour timeout and relieve your stress. Light some candles, put on some relaxing music, and soak away.

- **Body scrubbing**—Fill your sink with hot water. Using a terrycloth towel, hold both ends in your hands and dip the towel into the water. Wring it out and gently scrub one area at a time until your skin becomes pink. This can promote circulation, relieve stress, and calm your mind.

- **Foot soak**—Fill your tub or a wash basin or foot bath with the warmest water you can tolerate. Add a drop or two of your favorite essential oil, such as peppermint or lavender, and allow your feet to relax and release the weight of your world.

🕯 **Massage**—Treat yourself to regular massages at intervals that work for you. Finding a great massage therapist is a must. It should be one you can feel comfortable with and truly relax. You can even start by teaming up with a friend to do neck and shoulder massages on each other. If you have a special someone in your life, this can be a great way to connect. Massage can help relieve tension and increase circulation, making you feel relaxed and refreshed.

🕯 **Chiropractor**—I believe that regular chiropractic care is crucial to adjusting your overall balance and well-being. If you have never been, check it out. Many insurances will cover a limited number of visits each year. It is an alternative medicine that is well worth it.

🕯 **Organic clothing**—When you are cleaning out your closets and paring down, check your clothing labels. Are the majority of your clothes synthetic fibers? These fabrics tend to not allow your skin to breathe and this can impact the function of your lymphatic system. Choose comfortable clothing, cotton whenever possible, and organic cotton is best.

🕯 **Herbal teas**—Try a night-time routine of experimenting with a variety of delicious blends of herbal teas. Organic varieties are preferred because of their purity. A cup before bed can help you sleep, some teas can help detoxify your liver and also aid in your digestion. Drink it from a special mug or a teacup and saucer.

🕯 **Dark chocolate**—This one doesn't need explaining! Go ahead and indulge. Lots of research shows that dark chocolate has many health benefits. So sit and savor a piece or two.

🕯 **Daily stretch**—Incorporating a daily routine of stretching and/or meditating can be life changing. It allows you to get in touch with your inner self and your outer body. Being flexible and limber will help with your overall well-being. This can be done just before bed or first thing on rising. Go ahead and try it consistently for two weeks. It will become a habit that you won't want to break.

Many of these are similar for we all have basic needs. It is the how and why that is unique to each of us. If you are struggling with self-love and your self-care is suffering a bit, check out my website, www.kelly-kurtz.com, for your complimentary Health History Assessment and see how together we can add some sparkle and shine back into your life.

Simple Abundance

> *The simplest things are often the truest.*
> —Richard Bach

I find this to be so accurate. I am not sure if I always knew this and lost my way, or if I am finally figuring it out after coming full circle. It goes back to the "someday house" that I spoke of in Chapter 6. Wanting more, needing more, and the feeling that if I just had "this or that" then I would have it all. I would be happy, complete, and be living the dream.

As I have wandered along in my journey, I have realized it is less about the things that you own, and more about the relationships you cultivate. Less is more—downsizing, simple decor, and small-scale basics. I have worked hard to eliminate excess, reduce clutter, and see "stuff" as just "stuff." You can't take it with you wherever it might be that you end up when you leave this world.

Will you have piles and boxes and closets full of stuff for your loved ones to sift through when you are gone? When my mother passed, she had been relatively healthy while living with her cancer until the final two months or so. She believed she was going to be around for a while and wasn't sorting through any of her possessions. That would be a job for us once she was gone.

It was a weird and painful experience doing so. I was overcome with emotion as I opened her dresser drawers to see everything still there,it was as if opening her dresser drawers to see everything still there, as if she was just out running on an errand and would be right back. Her pocketbook was hanging on the hook in the hallway. Inside her wallet, complete with money unspent, was her driver's license, loose change, her favorite lipstick, and a few receipts—here one day and gone the next. We are here for really such a brief time.

As an occupational therapist, I have worked in acute rehabilitation settings. Often a patient who has suffered an injury or illness goes to the hospital and then ends up in rehab. They were out doing whatever, living their life, when an unfortunate event took place. Somehow they end up in rehab. We often ask the family to bring some clothing so that they can do their rehab in the therapy gym in something other than a hospital gown.

I often see the same thing when the clothing comes in. The patient says things such as, "Oh, why did you bring those pants, they are so uncomfortable?" or "That sweater is too tight and the fabric is really itchy. Out of all the things in my closet, you picked the stuff I never wear."

My point is if someone had to go into your closet right now without you being there or giving them specific instructions, could they pick out random clothing to bring to you that you would be happy and comfortable in? I am guessing most of you would say not 100 percent of the time. We have too much stuff. Life is too short to wear clothes we do not love, look great, and feel comfortable in. We hang on and hold on to stuff that we no longer want or need.

What is clogging up your physical space and in turn cluttering your mind?

_____

_____

What is one area you can commit to reducing the excess today, this week, this month? Go ahead, write it down. Committing to it on paper means you are more likely to actually achieve it.

Are you still stuck on how to get started? Contact me. I can help. "Simply Well. Simply Organized" is my business. It is a component of the health coaching services I offer. Imagine having a house that is clean and organized and is in alignment with your life's passion, purpose, and desires. There is such a thing as organized simplicity, and once you have it, you will have a fresh canvas to paint the tranquility, peace, and serenity back into your life. What's holding you back? Go ahead, its time.

She believed she could, so she did.
—Unknown

chapter 8
The Finishing Touches

So much of today's world is focused on perception. How we look or how we think we should look according to the media, social networking, and the constant comparison of ourselves to others. I think as we grow older into our forties, fifties, and beyond, we care less about being perfect and focus more on being happy. We are more comfortable in our own skin and the reality of looking like a supermodel just isn't practical.

Perhaps this is when the term "late bloomer" takes hold. We begin to see that time moves quickly and that we want certain things in our lives without a doubt, and yet we come to the realization that some things no longer serve us. Coming to this point is somewhat of a gradual transition for most people, but it can be a result of a sudden realization of the frailty of life. Either though losing a loved one or having a serious injury or illness ourselves can quickly change our perspectives.

In doing so, we begin to appreciate the simple everyday things more and truly see joy and pleasure in the simple abundance that already surrounds us. It is a glass half full versus a glass half empty. As your renovations continue to take hold, you will feel a shift in your energy. You might experience a light burning inside of you, keeping you focused and determined to continue on your way. Go ahead, blaze new trails, and trust your instincts to guide you.

Your Personal Soundtrack

I have a friend who went through a divorce a few years before I did, and one night I was visiting with her at her new home. She had some great music playing in the background as we were having a glass of wine. They were all random songs, or so I thought, but all were great. At first I asked her what radio station she was listening to because I was definitely going to make it my new favorite. She replied that she was simply playing the soundtrack of her life.

At first, I didn't understand what she meant, so I asked more questions. She had various playlists that contained all kinds of music—some happy, some sad, classical, rock, pop, country, and jazz. There was room for all of it. You see her life had had many chapters, like all of us. She realized the power of music and what role it had played in her past and present life. That evening as various songs came on, they reminded me of various things, people, places and memories of, good times, and some not-so-good times.

I had been using an iPod when I exercised and I often listened to the radio when I was in my car. The music I played could, and did, have a direct effect on my mood. Ironically, one stinking song could make me cry—make me sad and lonely for someone or something. It could remind me of a dark place or time in my life. Yet another song could have the exact opposite effect. What's on your playlist? Are you stuck in the same place because you keep replaying the past? How can you use music to move forward and embrace the present moment?

The Walk-in Closet

We talked briefly about our closets earlier in this book—organizing our clothes and paring down unwanted, out of style, or off-size clothing. How many people have three different sizes hanging inside their closets? The wardrobe that will look great on us if we just lose those last 10 pounds, the wardrobe from when we were 10 pounds heavier, and the basic stuff we wear every day.

Keeping the big stuff is a bad idea because that leaves the door wide open to return to that size if our inner voice returns and says, "You don't deserve to be thin." The stuff that is a few sizes too small is a constant reminder that you are not what you used to be and it ultimately makes you feel down on yourself.

The current stuff may not be great, because you tell yourself that you want to be thinner and when you get there, you will buy more clothes. I say live in the present in regard to your clothing. Now if you are really are in transition to a smaller size, by all means don't spend hundreds of dollars updating your wardrobe to then have to do it again in a month or two.

We all have seen pictures of classic women through the years. Those who come to mind for me include Audrey Hepburn, Catherine Deneuve, and Jacqueline Kennedy. They dressed in a clean, sharp, classic style that was to be admired and imitated, yet they each had an individual style about them as well.

What is your style? Do you have a look you find yourself going for again and again? Have you ever worn an outfit or a color that seems to get you endless compliments? If so, pay attention to that color or style. Chances are if people are noticing then they are on to something.

Years ago I had "my colors" done. My hair salon was hosting an opportunity to have your colors analyzed. Once they were done, you received a checkbook-sized case that contained different fabric swatches with your ideal colors. Each color had its own swatch and the intention was to carry this around in your purse so that when you were out shopping and found an item you wanted to buy, you were supposed to match it to one or several of your colors. It was fascinating to me.

As I began to buy and wear clothing that mirrored the colors in my book, I began to get complimented by random people, even strangers, who might say, "That shade goes splendid with your eyes," or "That jacket really brings out your skin tone." I also noticed that as I was purchasing items in my color family, that they began to coordinate with other items and therefore it seemed I had more wardrobe options, even though I didn't have many more items of clothing.

It was at that time that I really began to pare down my wardrobe. I started with basics of navy blue, brown, and black. I had pants and skirts in these colors and shoes that went with each outfit. I knew that I really only needed a few pairs of heels, some flats, and some casual-type shoes. I stuck to basic pieces, such as solid T-shirts, good quality, and nicely fitted. I had begun to build my wardrobe and started thinking about my clothing as an investment. I updated my bras and underwear. I replaced my socks and got rid of the ones that were worn or had holes. I finally tossed the mismatched ones that had been sitting in a basket patiently waiting to be claimed by its mate.

I took this concept and bought a few classic jackets and coats. I often waited until the off-season and got many items on sale. Knowing what color I was searching for made shopping so much easier too. As I learned my colors, I was able to add accessories, which is where my unique style comes in. I have some great costume jewelry pieces that can really make my outfits; I have scarves and belts that add a touch of individuality too.

In the process of adding pieces, I started getting rid of stuff—things that weren't comfortable, anything that had a stain or rip that couldn't be repaired. I got rid of my big clothes and some of my "skinny" clothes, although I was beginning to fit back into them.

I suggest you have a closet organization party. You can do this alone, but I recommend you get a friend to join you. A friend you love and who will be honest with you, and you won't get mad or offended when she tells you the jeans you love and think you look hot in actually aren't flattering. I am not suggesting throwing out all your clothes and going on a crazy shopping spree, good for you if you can, however, start small.

I like to organize my closet by color. I find it makes it easy to put together outfits and it allows me to find items quickly. It actually saves money too because I can see everything and I am less likely to buy a duplicate black sweater or my fourth pair of black slacks. You really can't have too many pairs of black pants. But, if you must, make sure you love them all! What style calls to you? Are there certain cuts of clothing that work well with your body type? If so, embrace them. Just because skinny jeans come in your size doesn't necessarily mean you have to wear them!

Do I Smell?

Do you remember when you were a teenager going into a department store with your friends and looking at the cosmetic counter? Maybe you got a free "makeover" or a sample of a perfume? How about all the index-sized cards in magazines that had scratch-and-sniff samples of the latest fragrances? We all know that "a little goes a long way." Maybe your mother told you that, I know mine did.

I have been in the grocery store minding my own business walking up and down the aisles (in fact, I am the only one in a particular aisle) yet I can smell the remnants of the woman who was there earlier. Her cologne hits me like a ton of bricks when I turn the corner, yet she is nowhere to be found. That is a little too much.

Every woman deserves to smell beautiful. What calls to you? Is it a soft, sweet, scented lotion or a clean, fresh, spritz of cologne? Do you prefer a dab at your pulse points and a smidge behind you ears? Whatever scent calls to you, keep it mysterious and use it sparingly. Like your wardrobe, your scent says a lot about you. It is meant to be noticed by those in your personal space or those you are intimate with, not everyone within ten feet of you.

There is something sexy about a man kissing a woman and being drawn in by her scent. This goes for your hair and skin too. Smelling nice makes you feel feminine and desirable, even if there is no one special in your life right now, but you. Caring for yourself and taking the time to nourish your body is a special way of telling yourself how much you are loved.

In Full Bloom

I hope you have discovered your own color palate and are adding some *Fresh Paint* to your life. Remember it is only paint. Keep your brush moving and expect touch-ups along the way! That way you can look in the mirror and smile at the person you've become!

You feel young at heart, no matter the age of your body. You are restored as you've learned about the incredible "you" who has been hiding under the surface for so many years.

Stand tall with your torch that you've carried through thick and thin, and celebrate the new you. You have redefined your purpose and learned ways to improve your self-care, embrace your health, and nourish your body and soul.

You have rediscovered your unique style and reclaimed peace, tranquility, and serenity in your life. Learn how to keep your brush moving and embrace and enjoy the simple abundance in your life.

Let me share with you a few words that mean a lot to me.

"I believe in Pink.

I believe that laughing is the best calorie
burner.

I believe in kissing,

Kissing a lot.

I believe in being strong

When everything seems to be going wrong.

I believe that happy girls

Are the prettiest girls

I believe that tomorrow is another day and

I believe in miracles."

—Audrey Hepburn

So, go ahead, you are ready to sparkle now!

Photographs by Steven S. Stearns

About the Author

When Kelly Kurtz turned 40, she finally realized the power that food had held over her health. She started really listening to the things her body was telling her. She connected her love of being organized and prepared with eating clean and healthy, and the rest is history.

As a holistic health and lifestyle coach, she is the founder of Simply Well. Simply Organized. She's deeply passionate about helping others get and stay organized and healthy.

One client described her as *Simply amazing with real life solutions*, while another declared her to be *a great teacher to get you organized and on a healthy routine, no matter how disorganized you are right now!*

Kelly has written about various health and wellness-related topics and has given many lectures and seminars on being healthy, eating well, and getting organized.

When she is not writing or speaking you can find her out on her bike, cycling the many roads of New England, taking yoga class, and spending time with her two amazing teenage children.

Meet Kelly and stay in-the-know about her upcoming happenings at www.kelly-kurtz.com.